STAGE DIRECTIONS

JOHN GIELGUD

STAGE
DIRECTIONS

RANDOM HOUSE

New York

792
636s
48666
Jan. '65

SECOND PRINTING

Printed in Great Britain by
Bookprint Limited, Kingswood, Surrey

CONTENTS

ACKNOWLEDGEMENTS

The author wishes to thank the Folio Society for permission to incorporate the chapter on *Richard II* which was originally published in the Folio Society edition of the play.

Thanks are also due to the owners of the photographs which are reproduced in this book. Acknowledgement has been made on the pages where the photographs are reproduced.

LIST OF ILLUSTRATIONS

INTRODUCTION

IN 1937, the year after my first appearance in *Hamlet* in New York, I wrote an account of my life up to that time. This book is not a sequel. In *Early Stages* I recalled my childhood, and tried to give some account of my distinguished family, especially the Terrys, on my mother's side, whom I knew and admired so much in their later acting years. But I found it more and more difficult, in the later part of the book, to avoid fulsome compliments, anecdotes and gossip about my contemporaries, and to try and write impartially about my own work.

So this book is rather more technical, and I hope more practical, though it does not pretend to be either a text book or a credo. My ideas and enthusiasms are still, I hope, comparatively flexible. Some of these chapters have already appeared in magazines, special editions, and interviews, and I acknowledge the courtesy of the publishers who have kindly allowed me to use some of the material again. But in every case I have rewritten considerably, in the hope of clarifying and avoiding repetitiousness as far as possible.

I consider myself to be a working actor. I have laboured for many years trying to learn and perfect my skill and craftsmanship, and I must be sure, when I come to tackle a part or a production for the first time, that I sincerely understand what I am about before I can hope to do it justice.

I have never understood politics or world affairs, and I am

lacking in ambition for power, large sums of money, or a passionate desire to convince other people that they are wrong and I am right; but I have a violent and sincere wish to be a good craftsman, and to understand what I try to do in the theatre, so as to be able to convince the people I work with.

Though I am inclined to be lazy-minded and ill-informed, I am thorough and industrious. I never stop trying to improve my work, but I am fearful of blind experiment and of seeming to display false intelligence in order to impress other people, or to branch out in a new direction unless I fully understand what I am doing. Long experience has perhaps made me unduly cautious, and I trust my own intuition with less confidence than I did when I was a young man. But I am, I believe, far more critical than I once was, less easily satisfied, more relentless in striving for selectiveness and simplicity.

I believe I can, as an actor, use words well, and, as a director, help others to deliver a text with variety and clarity. I know how to manage a scene on the stage so that the actors may convey to the best advantage what the author intends them to convey, but only if I fully understand, or feel instinctively that I apprehend, the author's motives and intentions.

But it is no use my pretending to be an intellectual where the theatre is concerned. I am, I hope, a professional. I try by what I do in the theatre to serve my author; to entertain an audience, arouse their interest, evoke their sympathy, passion, or hatred, to take them out of themselves, to enable them to pass three hours agreeably. If they can be moved, uplifted, amused or fascinated by what they have seen me do, I count myself happy – though not necessarily successful. I greatly enjoy planning, but dislike the practical details of theatrical finance and management. I love to work with authors, designers, musicians, and actors, and with the technical staffs of theatres, and, on the whole, I have been fortunate in my relationships over the years with people in all these different departments. On the rare occasions when I have had quarrels or found myself completely out of sympathy with certain individuals, I have been baffled and dismayed. I think I may say, without undue vanity, that on the whole I have been a good influence in the theatres where I have worked and in the plays with which I have been associated, and I am happier in this knowledge than in the occasional satisfaction I may have felt in the performances and productions of mine which have been considered to be popular and successful achievements.

But I cannot fail to be constantly aware of my own narrow limitations. For me the theatre has always been an escape, a make-believe world, full of colour and excitement, fun, emotion, poetry and movement, a world of striking characters and extraordinary personalities. I cannot bring myself to care for elaborate dialectic argument on the stage. Abstract plays have only appealed to me occasionally. I hate propaganda in the theatre, and I fail to understand how any play can hold an audience unless the experience of it is shared with at least a large majority of those watching its performance. Shapelessness, redundance, and acute class-consciousness irritate me profoundly.

I suppose it is natural, as I grow older, for me to find it difficult to repress a certain amount of nostalgia for the theatre of my youth – to check a feeling of resentment against the changes that have occurred, and must continue to occur, under the stress of modern conditions, in every branch of theatrical development. But I have learned, and have, I hope, much more to learn, from the younger generation of playwrights, directors, and especially the actors with whom I now come in contact for the first time.

Some of them, who chance to read this book, may find it somewhat old-fashioned in its point of view. Others may perhaps find some interest in it, if only as a personal expression

[xiii]

of opinions and experiences covering a period of years in which the theatre moved violently (though almost imperceptibly at first) into a completely new phase, impossible to imagine when I first entered the profession forty-two years ago.

ART OR CRAFT

I DECIDED to go on the stage in 1921. But I did not begin to be an actor until 1923. Till then I had only held spears, walked on, and studied at two different dramatic schools, where I was considered to be a talented but conceited pupil.

Schools, of course, do give one a certain preliminary discipline and sense of orderliness. They help the beginner to overcome self-consciousness, especially in working in classes with other students, which is apt to be very embarrassing at first. Above all, the influence of one really sympathetic teacher may be invaluable.

I had promised my parents that if I had not made good in the theatre by the time I was twenty-five I would try my hand at architecture. Actually, I hoped as a boy to become a stage designer. I was stage-struck, mad about the theatre. I thought I might perhaps follow in the footsteps of my second cousin Gordon Craig (Ellen Terry's son), whose books and drawings I so much admired, but feared I was too lazy and inefficient to learn the technical requirements of a stage designer –mathematics, blueprints, accurate drawing and so forth. I was lucky enough to be engaged by my cousin, Phyllis Neilson-Terry, who was taking a London success of hers on tour. In this play (J. B. Fagan's *The Wheel*) I stage-managed, understudied, and gradually began to learn to become an actor.

At first I tried to imitate the players I most admired,

particularly Claude Rains, who had been my teacher at the Royal Academy of Dramatic Art. I had seen him play Dubedat in *The Doctor's Dilemma*, and much admired his death scene, in which he wore a rich dressing-gown, and hung his hands, made up very white, over the arms of his wheelchair. Soon afterwards I understudied him in a play called *Robert E. Lee*, by John Drinkwater, and played his part a few times. Later, after a rather dreary Christmas season playing one of the dim young undergraduates in *Charley's Aunt*, I also understudied Noël Coward in his play *The Vortex*, and followed him in the part of Nicky when he left the cast. It seemed to me that the only way to say the lines was to imitate as nearly as possible the way he had said them, and this kind of mimicry led me into some rather mannered habits. Coward's style of speech and manner is not quite the same as mine, although my clipped vowels and rather staccato manner are not altogether unlike his. Perhaps in the twenties we all talked a bit like that. Coward, after all, was the angry young man of the day, and we all thought it smart to copy him.

Leslie Faber, a brilliant and underestimated player, who thought well of my potentialities and gave me much good advice in the short time I knew him before his death, once told me it took fifteen years to make an actor, and I believe it is not possible, even with unusual good luck and hard work, to achieve real skill in a shorter time. The setbacks I encountered in my early years were just as valuable to me as my few juvenile successes.

I suppose the most rewarding influence in my stage career has been the joy of discovering Shakespeare and working in his plays. Apart from this, I owe most to the inspiration of Harley Granville-Barker, who wrote me letters of encouragement and criticism over several years, though I was actually only directed by him on one occasion. Theodore Komisarjevsky, the Russian director, thought well of me too, and influenced me greatly, teaching me not to act from outside, seizing on obvious effects and histrionics; to avoid the temptations of showing off; to work from within to present a character, and to absorb the atmosphere and general background of a play. These were things I had never thought important before. He also gave me my first important lesson in trying to act with relaxation – the secret of all good acting. Young actors when they are nervous tighten up as soon as they try to convey emotion, and this tension can sometimes be effective for a few moments, though physically and vocally exhausting. Until I worked with Komisarjevsky I was always showing off, either in a romantic or hysterical vein, using these two styles alternately in parts like Dion Anthony, in *The Great God Brown* (by Eugene O'Neill), and Constantin Treplev, in Chekhov's *The Seagull*, tense young men who seemed to be not so very different from myself. Later, in 1931, I was to make my first real success in modern clothes in a very good contemporary part in a play called *Musical Chairs*, by a young author-friend of mine, Ronald Mackenzie, who died tragically soon afterwards. But this was after I had worked for two seasons at the Old Vic (1929–1930) and had played a succession of Shakespearian leading parts, and one or two supporting ones. It was then that I felt I really had begun at last to learn something about acting and its problems. As a boy I had always loved costume plays, especially the romantic fustian dramas so popular as vehicles for the actor-managers who were then nearing the end of their careers – my great-uncle Fred Terry, Sir John Martin-Harvey, Matheson Lang, Robert Loraine (especially in *Cyrano de Bergerac* and Strindberg's *The Father*), all fine bravura players whom I admired greatly. I longed to be dressed in velvet and silk, wave a hat about, fight duels, and make love to ladies on balconies. But after my Shakespeare seasons at the Old Vic, I began to be aware how immensely skilled an actor must be in order to project a character; to speak Elizabethan verse or prose and to wear costumes with conviction and authority.

I think that many young actors fail to understand what Shakespeare's language has to offer them. Good verse-speaking is rather like swimming. If you surrender to the water it keeps you up, but if you fight you drown. The phrasing and rhythm and pace should support the speaker just as water does a swimmer, and should be handled with the same skill, ease and pace. Of course, even in the most colloquial modern speech, there is also a pattern which the actor has to find, and if this is presented with individual skill and personality, the text will carry with greater variety and significance. In some ways, perhaps, modern dialogue needs to be given even more colour and tone than verse. In Shakespeare, provided you can control your breath and rhythm, the flow of the verse will help to sustain you, though you must be careful to keep control of the shape and not be tempted to put in too much expression.

A good actor should be skilful enough to adapt his means of presentation according to the demands and quality of the text on which he has to work. I always imagine that Henry Irving, when he put his performances in 'between the lines of Shakespeare', as Shaw said, must have achieved magnetic results at the expense of the poetry. But in plays in which the dialogue was only a second-rate framework for action, character, and situation, he knew how to illuminate it so that it appeared to be very much better than it really was. His greatest virtuoso performances were evidently improvised out of clumsy old dramas, and often rewritten at rehearsals and during revivals over many years, but they never failed in their effect upon his audiences. In the old days, actors sometimes had to invent a kind of pantomime of their own on the scenario of some sensational story and set of situations, just as the great variety entertainers, Beatrice Lillie, Danny Kaye and Chaplin can when they improvise today. In a fine classical text, on the other hand, the actor is surely only an instrument in an orchestra, and must contribute his solo or concerted share to it, executing it as correctly as possible. Bernhardt's greatness in *Phèdre* is said to have been as undisputed as her acting in *Camille* and the melo-dramas of Sardou.

Many modern actors, I believe, are inclined to think that Shakespeare must be spoken naturalistically at all costs. But when Shakespeare wants to be naturalistic he writes: 'Pray you, undo this button', 'Dost thou not see my baby at my breast that sucks the nurse asleep', 'All the perfumes of Arabia will not sweeten this little hand.' Such lines are extraordinarily simple, and every audience will find them moving. But they will only achieve their ultimate effect if they are supported by the rich scaffolding built so firmly round them in the speeches which precede and follow.

I try to study the sound, shape and length of words them-selves, so as to reproduce them exactly as they are written on the page. In a verse speech (and often in a long prose one too) I am constantly aware of the whole span of the arc – the begin-ning, middle and end of the passage. I try to phrase correctly for breathing, punctuation and emphasis, and then, conforming to this main line, I experiment within it for modulation, tone, and pace, trying not to drag out the vowels, elongate syllables, or pounce on opening phrases, and being very careful not to drop the ends of words and sentences and to pronounce the final consonants – D, T, P, and so forth.

A year or two ago I saw *The Connection*, the dope play, in New York, which created such a sensation. The performance was said to be intensely realistic and intimate. But the actors seemed to have no idea that the lines must be spoken in a way that would make them sound more interesting. No doubt the author and director were aiming at just this kind of monotonous realism. But it is not very rewarding for an audience to sit for a whole evening listening to dialogue delivered in the same unvarying tone of voice. They can hear such talk for nothing in a train, bus, or bar, or even in their own homes. Absolute realism is always effective at first, especially in a small theatre, and sometimes on the microphone too, where little projection is needed, but it is very limited in its power to sustain the interest of a restless audience for a whole evening in a large house.

I think an actor has to find his own especial way of working, selecting his effects from what he has found out for himself in all kinds of different experiments at rehearsals – experiments of movement, experiments of give-and-take with the other players – in order to gain the necessary flexibility to contribute to and fit in with the director's intentions as far as possible. I hope I am a fairly obedient pupil. If I agree to work under a director, I always try to do what he tells me, unless I feel strongly that he is not helping me at all, in which case I would probably resign from the part. Working with Granville-Barker and Harcourt Williams, with Peter Brook, Michel Saint-Denis and Komisarjevsky I have been especially happy in past years.

In choosing a role I am chiefly influenced, I suppose, by my instinctive interest in the character as I read the play – and the hope that I might perhaps interpret it better than anyone else could, and the feeling that my own personal limitations, physical and spiritual, might, in this particular case, find adequate means of expression; that the part might stretch me, even beyond my own expectations, through the desire I feel to undertake it.

Sometimes I read a play in which I am offered a new part, and suddenly I imagine, 'Oh, I believe I could do something with this.' It is usually a very instinctive feeling, and has nothing to do with understanding the details of the whole work. I suddenly see the way I am going to look, the way I am going to speak, the way I am going to move. If I did not imagine all this so vividly I would never dare to undertake it. This happened to me with all the great parts I played when I was at the Vic as a young man – Lear, Macbeth, Antony, Hamlet. In some cases, particularly in *Macbeth*, I had more success the first time than when I came to study the part more thoroughly twelve years later. I simply imagined it, and acted it for the main development and broad lines of the character, without worrying about the technical, intellectual, and psychological difficulties. I played it from scene to scene as it seemed to come to me as we rehearsed the play. With only three weeks, of course, there was not time to do much more than that. I think one should dare to fly high when one is young; one may sometimes surprise oneself. It is wonderful to be able to give the imagination full play, hardly realizing what an exciting danger is involved.

I am surprised that my limitations, in outlook, tastes, and experience, have not prevented me from achieving success in some of the great parts of Shakespeare. The joke is that people think of me as an intellectual actor. Yet I have always trusted almost entirely to observation, emotion and instinct. In the theatre, I cannot help being very emotional. I am less so in life or in everyday moments of crisis, when I believe I manage to restrain myself, and try to appear controlled and dispassionate. But the moment I go into a theatre, either as director, actor, or audience, I find emotion overcomes me almost too easily. Then I have to select from my emotional enthusiasms, and decide how to use only what can be selected to best advantage. I have only learnt through long experiment how to choose, out of three or four instinctive feelings, the one likely to be exactly significant for a certain scene and situation as I mean to play it.

Some actors, of course, are not at all intuitive, but I think the best ones always are. Fine acting casts a spell upon the whole audience, as the player himself knows at once by the silence and attentiveness of those in front. But it may also convey, to certain individual members of that audience, implications of which even the actor was not himself aware. The spontaneous association of the player with a character can sometimes even transcend his own deliberate planning and intention.

Of course acting is pretence, but it is also an art, or perhaps more correctly speaking a craft. It may be expressed in terms of poetry, realism or abstraction, just as a picture, music or sculpture may – but unlike these other arts, acting must necessarily always be interpretative, except in the case of clowns and improvisators. Therefore, the dramatic truth is the most important thing for the actor to find in a first-class text. With poor material he may sometimes find a different kind of truth – in melodrama or farce, for instance – and he has to find the right kind of truth and style for the particular kind of play in which he is taking part; a broad, larger-than-life kind for melodrama, a solemn yet light kind for farce. Sometimes too, he may insert his own 'actor's truth' in between the lines of a situation crudely fashioned for him by the author, and so embellish its effect. But this is a dangerous mistake when acting Shakespeare's plays. This was the reason for Shaw's continual disparagement of Irving's performances in Shakespeare, when he wrote so firmly to Ellen Terry, 'Play on the lines, within the lines. *Never* in between the lines.'

I think that images, of memories and past events, often help the actor's imagination. Stanislavsky talks a lot about image suggestions. In plays like *Richard II*, which have elaborate imagery in the writing, I have always tried at each performance to find the same implication, the same picture that came to me as I spoke the words at rehearsal for the first time. But even in the most elaborately conceived characterization I now realize,

[8]

as never before, how important it is that the quality of selectiveness be always kept in mind. The famous picture of the Van Gogh chair seems surprising when one sees it first, the strange angle, the brilliant colour. But after seeing that picture it is impossible to see a kitchen chair again without thinking of Van Gogh. His own particular view of it was strikingly original, and so personally felt that it affects one afterwards every time one sees a kitchen chair. In the same way an actor's most memorable effects are often brought about by the fact that he has felt a certain moment so individually. But once he has discovered how to execute this moment in his own particular way, he must be able to repeat each detail of it over and over again by technical means, either with the help of visual images (which may be his own private affair) or through his precise skill in emphasis and timing. He has learned through long experience exactly how certain results may be obtained. He may time something by accident during a performance which is suddenly rather effective, and afterwards perhaps he will find how to make it carry a little more certainly. A few people in the house will react to some look or gesture, but the actor is aware from the lack of complete stillness that it does not yet carry to the whole audience. Then he tries experiments of various kinds at each successive performance, spreading his effects a little more broadly, or closing them up if they seem too crude and obvious. And here lies the interest of long runs and the discipline of playing parts again and again; certain effects are found and tried, and yet these must always be controlled and related, at each separate performance, to the acting of the other players. For a certain method may succeed when playing a part with one group of actors, but not with another, since their reactions in the scene are not the same and therefore the whole timing and pace will have to be adjusted accordingly. Besides, the audiences are always changing. But with long experience the actor will also learn to leave

[9]

well alone, once he feels he has done enough in the way of experiment and selection.

The discipline of working in the theatre is not such an unpleasant responsibility to me now as it was when I was a beginner. In those days I was not very conscientious. I often played the fool on the stage, and would arrive at the theatre only just in time for the performance. Now I would not dream of committing those breaches of discipline, and I am very severe towards young people who are guilty of such behaviour. The time spent in making-up before every performance is also a valuable form of relaxation for the player. Of course make-up is not very fashionable nowadays, and a lot of people go on without any. But I always enjoy shutting myself in my dressing-room, sitting down at my table with my personal things around me and making-up (as I shave every morning) in a routine which becomes more and more mechanical as the run continues. It is good to take one's time to put on one's costume carefully, to go down on to the stage and hear the beginning of the play, knowing exactly the moment when it will begin and end. So different from the endless uncertainty of the film studio, when people have to sit about all day long and are then expected to spring into action for half an hour or so, only to be forced to wait again for an uncertain number of further tedious hours. The punctual routine of the theatre is a fine thing, though in a very long run it is an arduous effort to conform to it. The quality of audiences begin to deteriorate after a time, and the actors are apt to allow this to discourage them; they dread being asked to rehearse, though they know that is what they really need. During actual performances actors vary very much in their behaviour. Some can play the fool while they are in the wings and then go on for a scene and immediately burst into tears, shriek with laughter, or fall dead, with complete conviction. Others must not be spoken to at the side of the stage. They like to be left alone in order to concentrate before-hand. Some go through their whole part in the dressing-room every night before going on. One learns to observe and respect such varying habits in one's colleagues while one is working with them.

All players have their own rules for their life outside the theatre. For myself I always like to sleep for at least one hour, sometimes more, every afternoon. And I eat sparingly before I act.

Sometimes I think that actors ought to do preliminary exercises as dancers do. In Brendan Behan's play, *The Hostage*, some time ago, the cast was asked by Joan Littlewood to come in an hour beforehand to meet on the stage and take part in a kind of improvised sing-song, in the spirit of the play. This was rather a Brechtian device, and there may have been something in it, though I think it would embarrass me very much to do it myself. I try not to be wrapped up too much in the theatre when I am away from it, but I believe too that almost unconsciously I save myself all day for my performance.

Acting is never easy, though once I used to think so. After so many years, I find it sometimes an escape, occasionally a pleasure, more often a responsibility. I enjoy it most when I am acting with other players whom I admire and respect, and, of course, when the audience is particularly responsive. I never feel I have a part under control until I have played it in public for at least six weeks. After that I try to set my performance and to simplify rather than elaborate. I do not learn my lines by rote, until I have read with the company several times. Once I used to be a very quick study. Nowadays I have to write out my words in longhand, sometimes more than once, as I have a bad tendency to learn sense and rhythm with many inaccuracies of detail. I am quick to feel when cuts would improve my speeches, and occasionally I beg leave of a modern author to change the shape of a sentence if I feel the rhythm is easier spoken another way. When I am studying, I am subconsciously affected by everything I see and hear going on about me. The imagination is already geared to some of the implications of the character that is slowly being brought to life. I remember noticing a tramp lying face downwards, his face and hands buried in the dirty grass, on a sweltering day in St James's Park, when I was walking home from a rehearsal of *Crime and Punishment*. His spread-eagled, despairing abandonment was exactly that of Raskolnikov lying on his bed in his attic after the murder.

It is essential for an actor to acquire technique, though possibly, if he is lucky enough to be cast, early in his career, for a role in which his particular qualities are ideally suited, he may succeed without it.

I sometimes feel that I am a bit too fond of pleasing the audience. Yet they have come to enjoy themselves, or at least to be interested and stimulated in some way. How much should actors try deliberately to entertain? It is, of course, important that the public should not be bored, or go to sleep, or walk out. But I think if you once allow them to influence you too strongly, if you become too anxious for popularity and applause, audiences can easily cheapen your quality as an actor. They are often inclined to prefer your most obvious effects, and confuse the part of your personality which they themselves like best with the appropriate qualities of the character you are representing upon the stage. This happens very much in films, where a man like Brando, who is a thrilling artist, has been encouraged by the public to over-cultivate a kind of mannered technique which may prevent him from making the experiments that his great talents ought to have allowed him during his best acting years. It is a great temptation for a big star to keep to the particular vein which is most popular with his public. If he is given the opportunity, the real artist should sometimes attempt things in which he is not going to be quite so successful, or in which he may be surprised to find that he is more successful than he himself thought possible. He must not feel he has too much at stake in every venture. That is the great danger of becoming a valuable box-office personality.

Reality on the stage is never the same as reality in life, although it can seem to be so when it is successfully presented. In Chekhov's plays, of course, the action is very realistic, and I learned from Komisarjevsky to play 'with the fourth wall down', as we actors say, instead of using a more declamatory method of projection, as I would in Shakespeare. But I think that the difference is actually not so great as it appears to be. After all, even in Chekhov, the audience must still see the actors' faces. The characters must still sit facing the audience in many scenes. They must trick their faces so that they can be well seen and heard, and there are long speeches which, even in translation, must have variety of pace and rhythm, and subtleties of pauses and silent action which have to be marked distinctly both by the director and the actors. All this is just as difficult as reciting a great speech in Shakespeare, where you must face the public as much as possible, with the other actors below you and round you, to give the right space relationship and the reactions you need. I think that in so-called classical acting and in modern, colloquial acting you really have to apply the same rules; but in a realistic play you apply them in a rather more muted way, just as when you act in a film you must use a great deal less voice, and find yourself limited by a lot of tags and marks to keep you within range of the camera. You have to learn another completely new set of rules when you are recording for the gramophone, and in this medium you find you can handle a speech with a quite different speed and modulation from the way you spoke it in the theatre. In television again there is a fresh set of rules. I think it is harder for young actors today to master so many different techniques than in the old days when they only needed to learn the craftsmanship of the living stage.

Fortunately none of the new forms of entertainment – movies, T.V., recording and radio – can do without trained stage actors. Unfortunately, on the other hand, professional players, especially if they are not very young, can easily sound (and look) mannered and false until they have mastered the different technical conditions of the new media. A young natural voice is often strikingly effective for a few moments – especially on radio or T.V. – because it is actually more spontaneous than the voice of an actor of skilled experience. The trained actor may easily seem too solemn, pompous, and unreal. This is the great difficulty also in speaking Shakespeare on the stage. The words must somehow be conveyed with a fine point of truth so that they are not just sound for its own sake. And yet in some of the great Shakespearian speeches, Cleopatra's mourning over the body of Antony, for instance, it is more important to find the richness and pattern of the sound rather than to stress the meaning or the sense.

Speech and silence are the two most powerful factors of the living theatre. Their basic values have been distorted, in this extraordinary mechanical age, by the new inventions – the gramophone, transistor set, television, by amplification both in the theatre and the cinema. People live with a perpetual background of noise, and it seems that many welcome such an accompaniment to prevent themselves from feeling lonely and dissatisfied with the monotony of their daily occupations. Often, however, they do not really listen. They merely become insensitively accustomed to some kind of sound vaguely continuing in their vicinity. Consequently, in the theatre, it has become more difficult to catch their interest with the subtle orchestration of living actors' voices and personalities, just as it is more difficult to emphasize for their benefit the significant look or vital moment of action, when they are lazily used to the forceful device of the close-up on the screen. The problem of projecting a subtle play in a large theatre is more challenging today than ever before.

2

DIRECTING THE CLASSICS

SEVEN OR EIGHT of Shakespeare's plays are very familiar to me – too familiar perhaps.[1] I find it difficult to read them freshly without confusing my impression of the characters with the performances of certain actors in productions which I have already seen; in fact, to approach the play as I would a brand new manuscript.

It is not difficult to discover, with the help of the scholars and commentaries, what the actual words mean, where cuts may be sanctioned, how the act waits may best be placed. But one cannot digest too many outside opinions, and it is always dangerous in the theatre to substitute scholarship and critical opinion, however brilliant, for contemporary instinct and fresh, vital imagination.

I find it hard to work in detail before beginning to work with the cast of a play I am to direct, and I have never been altogether convinced that completely meticulous preparations beforehand can ever be entirely satisfactory. Until the day when all the participants meet together to begin the work, theory and planning, even on paper, can be no more than a daydream. Yet the impression created in one's imagination, after reading the play through several times, must be the foundation of one's work as a director. Unfortunately this impression is likely to be

[1] See Appendix 2

extremely nebulous, yet I believe one should try to fix it in one's mind as a basic start. I mean that the play must be continually developed from what one conceives, in reading it, to be the sound and texture of the words, the movement and development of the action, and the kind of physical and pictorial atmosphere that seems to be demanded by the author.

Of course the whole question of direction in the theatre is a highly controversial one. All through theatrical history, the most gifted and successful actors achieved unique popularity and subsequent fame by their individual virtuosity. No one will ever know if they were helped or hindered by advice and criticism, or what suggestions they demanded or accepted from those they worked with at rehearsals. Performances of the great characters of Shakespeare, as interpreted by virtuoso players, and handed down to us in the accounts of Pepys, Lamb, Hazlitt, Shaw and Beerbohm, Archer and Walkley, have preserved Shakespeare's reputation in our theatre, I suppose, more surely than any so-called 'direction' of his plays, however well conceived. Indeed, the very name 'director', replacing the more utilitarian office of stage manager which preceded it, is of quite recent origin in the sense in which we understand it now.

It is no use planning the shape and balance of a production if the director does not consult the leading players to some considerable extent. By failing to do so, he may easily lose the invaluable confidence and help that he might otherwise gain from their co-operation. Their opposition or conflicting personal views may not only blow his own schemes sky high, but may also affect the loyalty of the other actors.

And yet one does not wish to discuss one's ideas beforehand with too many people, or to have too many outside opinions confusing or conflicting with one's own. At the same time it is of enormous advantage to work for a manager or impresario whose opinion one respects, and who is capable of giving practical advice in moments of rehearsal crisis. Also it is a relief (at any rate to me) to have the whole of the financial side of theatrical business taken care of by someone who is an expert in such matters.

Actor-managers who ran their own theatres in the past used to give long contracts, created their own personal policies, and frequently directed their own plays as well as acting in them. (Such were the theatres of Phelps and Irving, of Tree and Alexander, Hare and Wyndham, the Bancrofts and the Kendals.) Towards the end of the actor-managers' autocratic reign, the authors began to demand a greater share of responsibility and the right to handle their own plays themselves. Shaw, Pinero, and Barrie usually wrote with a particular cast in view, and the two former men directed many of their own plays. Granville-Barker, a man of genius and versatility, was highly gifted both as actor and author, but especially as a director. Dion Boucicault, Charles Hawtrey, and Gerald du Maurier were all better known to the public of their day for their successful acting achievements, but they were also famous within the profession for their skill as masterly directors and admirable managers.

The actor who is also a director is necessarily in rather a special kind of position, working in his double capacity. Provided he is at one with the author, he has the advantage of being able to develop his own strong feeling about the play without question or argument, since his authority will be undisputed in every department of the preparations. Then, too, he may understand his colleagues better, their moods and vanities, because he is himself an actor. He may allow them greater liberty to improvise, and is well equipped to deal with their moments of obstinacy or carelessness, their flashes of inspiration or despair. On the other hand, he may become too easily

ate I   SIR JOHN GIELGUD

Plate 2   LEONTES, with Mamillius (Robert Anderson)
in *The Winter's Tale*
Phoenix Theatre 1951

impatient with their technical deficiencies as compared with his own actor's skill, and be tempted to try to make them imitate him slavishly, forcing inflections on them, or showing them up by caricaturing their efforts. If they still fail to satisfy him, he may be tempted to cut the text, or try to cover the weaknesses of certain players with showy distractions of movement or business which he may invent, thus altering the balance of scenes so as to draw the audience's attention away from certain moments in the play which can never be achieved successfully, he thinks, with the material at his disposal. Time is short, the play is cast and in rehearsal. It is a great temptation to bully the players of the smaller parts who dare not answer back, and to flatter the leading actors by giving them their heads.

The ideal director of Shakespeare needs to have remarkable gifts besides the fundamental qualities of industry and patience. He should, of course, have sensitivity, originality without freakishness, a fastidious ear and eye, some respect for, and knowledge of, tradition, a feeling for music and pictures, colour and design; yet in none of these, I believe, should he be too opinionated in his views and tastes. For a theatrical production, at every stage of its preparation, is always changing, unpredictable in its moods and crises. Every person concerned in it has a different attitude, a different problem. Players of tried skill sometimes have to be toned down in order to balance and harmonize with those of lesser accomplishment, while the less experienced may need encouragement in order to gain greater confidence and style. There must always be room to adopt an unforeseen stroke of inventiveness, some spontaneous effect which may occur at a good rehearsal and bring a scene suddenly and unexpectedly to life. Yet the basic scaffolding must be firm, the speech modulated, clear, and varied, the phrasing elegant and clear, unaffected, constantly varying in pace and pitch. The movements should be simple (or apparently so), and calculated to put each speaker in the best possible position, so that the eyes of the audience are drawn inevitably towards him at the right moment. The positioning and grouping, in stillness or movement, in distance-relationship, should continually help the audiences to concentrate on the all-important words.

What the director cannot contribute, but the players can, is the life of the play; that is, the reality of the situation and its effect (or failure of effect) upon the audience. And so, it seems to me, the actors must always be considered first and last.

For a director is not in the same position as an orchestral conductor – though he may seem to be so at rehearsals, and the more inspiring his influence during this critical period the better. But when the play comes at last to be performed, and everything depends on the contact between the actors and the audience, the director is no longer presiding over the stage. His work is over now, and if the actors fail him (to say nothing of the electricians and stage management) he will have worked in vain. So the performers must not be so dependent on him that they are lost without him. His control over everything – scenery, lighting, music, acting, grouping, speaking – may have been brilliant or inept, but the final responsibility rests with the players once the curtain has risen and the audience is in their seats.

Actors need hints on carriage, diction, manner – and especially motive, though it is the character 'for their purpose' that usually interests them most, the character they have privately conceived. They may sometimes, at rehearsal, convince the director that he must change the whole balance and arrangement of a scene. A player may now feel he will appear to better advantage if he stands still while the others move, even though, in studying the scene beforehand, it had seemed essential to the director that the others should

be still and he should be the one to move. Every scene and character may be remoulded continually in rehearsal to suit the
actors, provided the basic mood and shape of the main conception is not destroyed or blurred by doing so. Endless varieties
of groupings and movements are possible. To change continually in rehearsal is not, to my mind, necessarily a fault on
the part of a director, though actors often resent it, and it is
generally considered to be one of my besetting sins. Of course
it tries the nerves of the actors if changes are continually
demanded of them till the very last rehearsal, but I feel it is
never too late to improve and alter – and especially to simplify –
even when a play has been running for many weeks.

There has already been a complete revolution in the acting
and directing of Shakespeare over the last fifty years. At the
turn of the century, William Poel's experiments and the books
and designs of Gordon Craig led the way to Granville-Barker's
Shakespeare seasons at the Savoy, just before the 1914 war,
when he built a modified apron on to the existing proscenium,
with runner curtains alternating with simple, stylized, semi-
permanent settings, decoratively designed by Albert Rutherston
and Norman Wilkinson. Later, the permanent set 'with variations' began to come into more general use, in Shakespearian
productions by J. B. Fagan and Bridges-Adams, achieving
greater speed and economy, and elaborate academic picture
scenery gradually became a thing of the past.

In my own productions at the New and Queen's Theatres, in
the nineteen-thirties, I hedged uneasily between various styles
of presentation, and only once, in *Romeo and Juliet* in 1935,
did I achieve, with the help of Motley who designed the production, something of a successful balance, at once picturesque,
speedy and varied, in the use of the stage space. My second
Hamlet production in 1939 (designed also by Motley for outdoor
performances at Elsinore but seen in London previously at

the Lyceum before it ceased to be a theatre) was, though Elizabethan in intention, a compromise in playing space, with intermediate scenes played on a long narrow apron in front of billowing traverse curtains, and cramped like a booth at a fair. We should have had the courage to build an upper stage and also a real apron of the right Shakespearian proportions.

Robert Atkins (who had begun with Tree) should be given great credit for his many admirable productions at the Old Vic in the twenties (in several of which I walked on as a super), especially as he achieved his remarkable results with an absolute minimum of time and money. Harcourt Williams, an equally dedicated artist (trained in his career as an actor by Benson, Ellen Terry and Barker), under whose direction I worked so happily in 1929 and 1930, followed Atkins at the Vic working on similar lines, with little money, admirable taste, and selective discrimination. Both men served the theatre with real integrity of purpose, modestly giving place to their successors, Tyrone Guthrie, Anthony Quayle, Michael Benthall, Glen Byam Shaw and Peter Brook, all of whom, working over the last twenty or thirty years both at the Vic and Stratford-on-Avon, have brought their respective talents to bear in different ways on developing style, speed and originality in their many brilliant Shakespearian productions. Today the permanent set with variations, the house curtain only dropped once or twice during the performance, and the playing of an almost full text – innovations unheard of at the beginning of the century – are now taken for granted by audiences.

Despite many fundamental improvements in the general scheme of technical presentation, however, I do not think any really basic solution to the playing of Shakespeare has yet been found during my forty years as an actor and thirty as a director. Of course the players and actors of each new generation need to rediscover Shakespeare in terms of their own particular time. Hence the freakish tendencies between the two wars – the modern dress productions under Barry Jackson in the twenties (not wholly unsuccessful, and useful in breaking many of the old traditions), and Komisarjevsky's experiments at Stratford-on-Avon, which were the more remarkable, since he achieved them with not more than a couple of weeks' rehearsal, and covered the weaknesses of such a shameful emergency by devising brilliant accompaniments – music, décor and panto-mime – to keep them spinning along, even though the plays themselves had not been properly rehearsed. This kind of experimental novelty rightly attempted to encourage con-temporary audiences to take a new interest in the plays. But the dignity and lucidity of true poetic style in diction, the balance and rhythm in declamation or soliloquy, the sword play and dancing, the deft juggling with words, pace and mood, whether in verse or prose, the infinite skill and variety needed to bring the genius of the plays to life, all these important ingredients are seldom given sufficient time and care. A com-pany is collected at random and trained to a necessary minimum of efficiency in four hectic weeks. Such conditions are simply not good enough to serve a great play worthily. In a concert hall no audience is expected to tolerate an orchestral perfor-mance of a classical work played by inexperienced executants. Yet how seldom has one ever been able to see a Shakespeare play with more than two or three of the parts played really brilliantly, or without several fatally weak performances among the supporting cast.

Now let us suppose the play is chosen, the actors cast, the main lines of production planned with the designers, the music and stage effects in hand. The company is gathered for the first reading of the play, and the director must now decide how he will begin the work in order to communicate something of what he feels himself, and hopes to bring to life, with their help, in the ensuing weeks. I myself believe it is unwise to deliver a long lecture at this early stage of the proceedings. The models and costumes have been brought by the designer, and the actors look at the drawings for the scenery perfunctorily – they will have their backs to it anyway, and entrances and exits are their only immediate preoccupation. But they probably examine the costume designs more carefully, and one sees the leading players making an immediate mental note of the dresses which they cannot (or will not) wear.

The reading begins, and the younger members of the cast try to listen obediently to the scenes that do not concern them, while the principal players either mumble apologetically or declaim uncertainly, suspecting the unspoken criticism of their colleagues. Irving was accustomed to read the play aloud, taking every part, and this, says Ellen Terry, was a great and inspiring experience for the company. Shaw was also a superb reader of his plays, but I know of no actor, author, or director today (not even Noël Coward) who would attempt to inflict such an ordeal upon his company. The readings of a Shakespeare play should, of course, in theory, be as important and constructive as the action rehearsals, but personally I have never found them very satisfactory. It is hard to hold the attention of a large company when the urgency of staging a play is in question, and the leading players long to make their first experiments alone with the director. They are too self-conscious to read and stop and argue theoretically, though lately, in the so-called *avant-garde* theatres, discussions among the players and long harangues by the director appear to have become the fashion.

Personally I prefer to have only one or two readings, and then slowly to begin to place the scenes. There will be time later on to sit down and study the pace and sound of individual passages in greater detail with one or two actors separately, after the main lines of the production are beginning to take shape. Every director has to choose the method that seems to him to give the best and quickest results, and his actors most confidence, for there is always the race with time to be considered. What then is the most efficient way to guide a company of players, supposing that the director is satisfied (as he seldom is) with the main pattern of the action that he has devised beforehand?

First the question of speech. He must criticize affectation, inaudibility, lack of feeling for musical shape, wrong inflections, a tendency to excessive declamation on the one hand or too great naturalism on the other. Next the cadence of speech, for in Shakespeare rhythm and sound can often be as important as they are in singing. A stylized projection of manner and voice must not be used inflexibly. An actor who begins a speech in heroic style must be able to swiftly change (as Shakespeare's words so often do) to a sudden appearance of simplicity. There must be constant variety of pace and tone, stillness in repose, liveliness in attack. In comedy, especially, the physical distance between actors is very important, and the director should experiment continually to make the best possible use of it. The audience needs time to appreciate points between the exchanges in the text, while the ball, just as in a game of tennis, is bandied expertly from one character to another and back again. Comedy 'points' can so often only be achieved by the give-and-take of both actors in a duologue – one offers the saucer, the other puts his cup on it.

Instinct is perhaps one of the most unpredictable and exciting qualities of really good acting, and I think it is often a mistake when actors try to approach their work too intellectually. I have known indifferent actors who can talk quite brilliantly on the craft of acting, and fine actors whom I have heard talk great nonsense about it too.

Of course no director can hope to drive his actors beyond a certain degree of accomplishment. But once the audience is present as a kind of sounding-board, he may begin to correct the balance of his production once again, and may even find it possible to develop the actors' performances further, though there is always the danger that they will prefer to elaborate rather than to simplify. Laughter and applause breed constant danger. The actors tend to forget the essential background mood of a scene through their interest in developing little points of detail. To insist on a false effect of pace may only result in producing an artificial vivacity – the thought must always precede the word. On the other hand, too much naturalistic pausing (to appear to be looking for the word or phrase) can easily be overdone, and produces an effect of dragging and portentousness. Long runs develop a fatal tendency to mechanical repetition. It is in the first few weeks of a run that actors are at the most sensitive in reaction, when they themselves are still fresh from the director's hand, and the audiences responsively at their best. Later, when the quality of the audiences begins to deteriorate, the performances on the stage will begin to slacken too, and the director will have to work hard to restore the necessary balance.

Changes in a cast are frequently necessary during a very long run, and though replacements can seldom hope to fit into the pattern which is already achieved to the complete satisfaction of everyone concerned, the necessity of rehearsing the play again nearly always brings fresh possibilities to light. In reviving an old production, or rehearsing a play already done in London for a new production elsewhere, on the Continent, say, or in America, I do not like to use my old prompt books in order to repeat moves and business with mechanical accuracy. If the same scenery is to be used again, there is naturally a certain amount of positioning which will be the same in a second version; but to say at rehearsals, 'This is when we get a big laugh by doing so and so' is an extremely dangerous way to go to work, and kills the whole impetus of a new company. It is sometimes hard to revive one's own enthusiasm for a production, however successful originally, that has become too familiar through many months of playing. In my last revival of *Much Ado About Nothing*, in New York, I felt my own spark was no longer lively enough to spur the company to the very best possible result – and the perfection of the ensemble in *Love for Love*, in London, seemed to me to put the company, which I afterwards took to New York in the same play, at a disadvantage, although, taken individually, one or two of the performances seemed to me actually better in America.

It seems to be easier to improve one's work in directing a contemporary play. In *Five Finger Exercise*, though the company, with only one exception, was the same as in London, the New York production gained considerably by fresh rehearsals and the background of a different set. Working again on the play, after a year's run in England, the actors were difficult to manage at first and reluctant to make the effort to revise their performances. The play opened to rather a lukewarm reception at Wilmington, and the company began to lose confidence and became alarmed. But the author, who was fortunately with us, suddenly saw a way of adding a few extremely valuable lines to the end of the first scene, and rewrote entirely the first ten minutes of the play, which I restaged completely while we were trying it out for a week in Washington, and this, I believe, contributed greatly to the excellent reception we received afterwards in New York. This shows that one is never really finished with work in the theatre, and how valuable it is to persevere and experiment continually.

3

KING RICHARD THE SECOND

RICHARD THE SECOND is a ceremonial play. In spite of its long list of characters only a few are of the first importance, and most of these are very broadly treated, especially in the early scenes. The young King himself, though his personal beauty and the subservient manner in which he is treated, as he sits idly on his throne, must draw all eyes to him immediately, is only lightly sketched at first in a few rather enigmatic strokes. It is not until after his return from Ireland, almost halfway through the play, that his inner character begins to be developed in a series of exquisite cadenzas and variations. In these later scenes, the subtleties of his speeches are capable of endless shades and nuances, but (as is nearly always the case in Shakespeare) the actor's vocal efforts must be contrived within the framework of the verse, and not outside it. Too many pauses and striking variations of tempo will tend to hold up the action disastrously and so ruin the pattern and symmetry of the text.

The actor of Richard cannot hope at any time during the action to be wholly sympathetic to the audience. Indeed he must use the early scenes to create an impression of slyness, petty vanity, and callous indifference. But he must also show himself to be innately well-bred, sensitive to beauty (as *he* understands it, though he cannot himself see the beauty of the dying Gaunt), lonely in his remote position of Kingship, young, headstrong, frivolous, and entirely out of sympathy with the older men who try so vainly to advise him and control his whims.

In the later scenes, however, the lovely lines he has to speak can hardly fail to win a certain sympathy for him, and he gradually becomes more understandable and so more pitiable. But owing to his utter lack of humour and his constant egotism and self-posturing, there is always a risk that he may become tedious and irritating to the audience unless the finer shades of his character are very subtly portrayed.

It is essential for an actor playing Richard to find the exact line of his disintegration. First, by grading the successive scenes as they follow one another, with their shifting changes of mood expressed in a continually minor key, and then by developing the detail and constructive pattern of the speeches as they become more elaborate and involved.

Richard is one of the rare parts in which the actor may indulge himself, luxuriating in the language he has to speak, and attitudinizing in consciously graceful poses. Yet the man must seem, too, to be ever physically on his guard, shielding himself, both in words and movement, from the dreaded impact of the unknown circumstances which, he feels, are always lying in wait to strike him down. He is torn between the intrinsic weakness of his nature and the pride and fastidiousness of his quality and breeding. He strives continually to retain his kingly dignity, to gain time by holding it up to the light before his enemies (as he will actually hold up the mirror later on in the deposition scene), while he prepares inwardly to face the shock of the next humiliation. Finally, cast out into the empty darkness of his prison, he is forced to realize at last that neither his personal beauty nor the divine right of kingship can save him from inevitable horror, as he is forced to contemplate his private doom.

Thus the actor has a dual responsibility. He must present the external action as the King suffers his defeats – the news of his favourites' deaths, the surrender to Bolingbroke at Flint, the defiant shame of the deposition scene and the agonies of farewell to his Queen. Yet he must somehow contrive at the same time to execute the poetic intricacies of the text with a full appreciation of its musical intention, using a completely lucid (and possibly stylized) method of vocal and plastic interpretation. The speaking of blank verse can only be projected, so as to hold an audience, by artificial and technical means – tone, emphasis and modulation. The task may seem an impossibly difficult one – to play, as it were, in two different styles at once, just as a singer has to do in opera. But this is actually a question of technique. A good actor experiences emotion at rehearsal – or imagines the experience of it vividly, which is not quite the same thing – and then selects, through trial and error, what he wishes to convey at each given moment of his performance. So he has always a double task – that of living in his role and at the same time judging his own effects in relation to his fellow players and the audience, so as to present an apparently spontaneous, living being, in a pattern carefully devised beforehand, but capable of infinite shades of colour and tempo, and bound to vary slightly at every performance. The actor is, after all, a kind of conjuror, and in a part like Richard he will find infinite opportunities to put his skill into practice, playing, as Richard himself plays, on the feelings of an audience until they are at one with the complicated nature of the character; then, even when they cannot condone his actions or sympathize with his misfortunes, they come at length to understand his intricate nature and can share in his unique experience.

Whether the scenes of the Aumerle conspiracy in the fourth act should be retained or omitted in the theatre is a difficult question to decide. Many people think that they are not by Shakespeare, and that they may have been cobbled together by another hand to pad out the necessary playing time, when the deposition scene, owing to its dangerous political implications, was omitted in Elizabeth's day. Certainly the rhyming couplets in these scenes have a strong flavour of fustian melodrama, and many of the lines can seem ridiculous unless they are delivered with consummate power and tact. Also they make the play considerably longer. On the other hand they are of value to vary the somewhat monotonous tone and style of the main part of the text, and they serve to make a break in style, dividing the two great scenes of Richard's grief (the deposition scene and the farewell to the Queen) from his final soliloquy and fight to death in the prison. These episodes gain considerably in their effect if the King has been absent from the stage for two scenes beforehand. Also, of course, the Aumerle scenes contain the celebrated passage between York and his Duchess, describing Richard's entry into London in the power of Bolingbroke, and the first references to the wildness of Prince Hal.

The opening scene of the play, though dramatically effective in reading, always presents considerable difficulties for a modern audience. The implications of the King's complicity in the murder of Gloucester (which has taken place before the action begins) are not easy to understand. Most of us are less familiar with history than the Elizabethans, who seem to have had a curiously detailed knowledge of the intricate topical events of the times chronicled by Holinshed and so faithfully followed in the Histories of Shakespeare. The opening quarrel between Mowbray and Bolingbroke is repeated with greater elaboration and formality in the tournament scene at Coventry, with only the short duologue between the Duchess of Gloucester and Gaunt to separate them. This intermediate scene also refers back almost exclusively to the murder of Gloucester, and it is difficult to make it interesting, since the Duchess appears without any introduction and is to have no further part in the action, though the account of her death some scenes later makes an effective moment for old York. In all this early part of the play the action is formalized and lacking in progression. The King's motives seem to be deliberately understated, while the characters of his Queen and various lords and favourites are very baldly indicated. Ceremony and fine speaking must combine to hold the interest of the audience. The vocal effects must be carefully orchestrated: Mowbray's fine tenor speeches, Bolingbroke's strong blustering tones, and the deep bass warning voice of Gaunt.

Unfortunately, throughout the tragedy, the verse seems to be too evenly distributed, and often with more music than sense of character. Everyone speaks in images, parentheses, and elaborate similes, whether gardeners, exquisites, or tough realistic nobles, and though this richness of metaphor gives, in reading, a beautiful, tapestried, somewhat Gothic effect (like an illuminated missal or a Book of Hours), the continually artificial style tends to become somewhat indigestible on the stage, and stands between the audience and their desire to get on more intimate terms with the characters and situations. It is therefore especially important to have actors for the chief parts who are strongly contrasted individual types as well as skilled speakers of verse.

The more simply the characters are played on broad, conventional (but not too melodramatic) lines, the scenes appearing to flow smoothly and swiftly with the correct stress and phrasing, but without too much elaboration, either of action, grouping, or pauses, the better will the beauty of the general pattern emerge and the interest of the audience be sustained. The actor of Richard may then be allowed, like the solo violin in a concerto, to take certain liberties with his cadenzas, developing their intricacies legitimately in an almost unlimited variety of pace and detail, in contrast to the more plodding ground bass of Bolingbroke, Northumberland and the other nobles.

Many of the shorter scenes in the play can produce an exquisite effect; especially the famous episode of the Queen with the gardeners at Langley, for example, and the little duologue between the Welsh captain and Salisbury (which has something of the same sensitive yet sinister effect as the little scene in *Macbeth* in which the murderers wait for Banquo on the lonely heath). These passages should have a romantic, simple expressiveness in contrast to the formality of the great scenes which precede and follow them.

There are several difficult links in the action. The scene between Ross, Willoughby and Northumberland after Gaunt's death, and the passage when the three favourites part for the last time on hearing of Bolingbroke's return, seem almost like choral exercises for three voices, and should, perhaps, be directed mainly from this point of view. The quarrel of the peers, before the entrance of Richard in the deposition scene, is difficult to stage without a dangerous risk of seeming ridiculous (the throwing down and picking up of gloves and so on), and it is advisable to make some discreet cuts to avoid bathos both here and in the Aumerle conspiracy scenes, if they are included. The character of York, used by Shakespeare as a kind of wavering chorus throughout the play, touching yet sometimes absurd, can be of great value, provided that the actor and director can contrive between them a tactful compromise between comedy and dramatic effect. To make him a purely farcical character (as has sometimes been attempted) weakens the play, and is quite opposed, it seems to me, to the intention of the dramatist. The women in the cast are very lightly drawn, and they are difficult parts for actresses to clothe with flesh and blood, though vocally and pictorially they can make a considerable effect – the two Duchesses old and proud, the little Queen so young and helpless – in the somewhat conventional episodes allotted to them.

Most of the characters, except Gaunt, York, Carlisle and the two Duchesses, seem to be young and full of life, and there should be something of the same impetuous brilliance that is so wonderfully vivid in *Romeo and Juliet* in the way they glitter and struggle and hurl themselves towards their fates. *Richard the Second* is a play, above all, which must in performance be finely orchestrated, melodious, youthful, headlong, violent and vivid. It must not be heavy or dragging, and the actors must know where they are going in their long speeches. Every effort must be made to contrast scene against scene. At first we must be made aware of the lightness of Richard's character, his fatal, obstinate frivolity, unchecked by the baleful warnings and implacable nobility of Gaunt. Then, as we reach the heart of the play, and the King's own heart and soul are gradually revealed to us by Shakespeare, we must see him forced, by the realization of his favourites' deaths and the desertion of his countrymen, reluctantly beginning to abandon his contemplative poetic fantasies, to face the brutal reality of Northumberland's hostility and the grim determination of the ruthless Bolingbroke.

The great problem, as in all Shakespearian plays, is to achieve a straightforward musical rendering of the verse, and yet to combine this with a sense of exciting actuality in the action. The events of the play must really seem to happen, and yet, as in an opera, the music of the lines must be neither slurred, dragged nor unduly hurried. In short, the technical brilliance of the poetic writing must be correctly balanced and simply executed, with the added colour of character and personality, while at the same time the shock of the actual events presented

Plate 3

ANGELO
in *Measure for Measure*
Stratford-on-Avon 1952

CASSIUS
with Brutus (James Mason)
in the film of *Julius Caesar*
M.G.M. 1950

M.G.M.

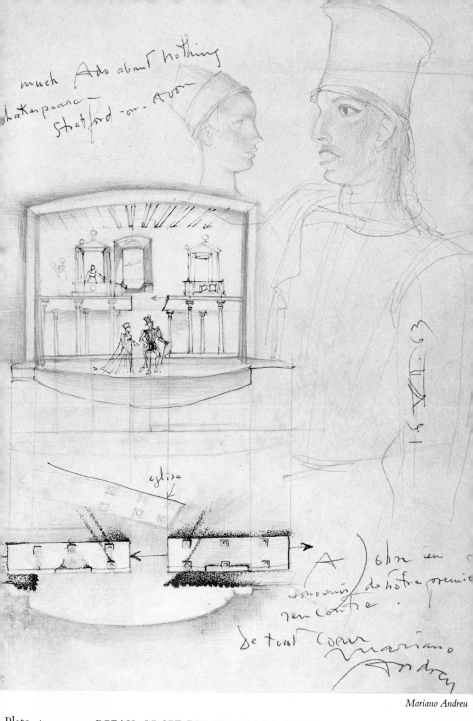

Mariano Andreu

Plate 4   DETAIL OF SET FOR MUCH ADO ABOUT NOTHING

(See p. 40)

must appear to be spontaneous and realistically convincing. The poetry must be welded imperceptibly into the dramatic action to a point where the audience will accept the two together – and, if successfully managed, the two styles should support one another to create a complete harmony of effect.

4

BENEDICK - LEONTES - CASSIUS

An OUTSTANDINGLY SUCCESSFUL production of a classical play can kill that play's popularity for many years afterwards. So it happened in England with *Much Ado About Nothing*.

Henry Irving produced the play at the Lyceum Theatre in 1882, with himself as Benedick and Ellen Terry as Beatrice, and afterwards revived it several times during his twenty years of management in London, besides touring it in the English provinces and in America. Ellen Terry presented it again under her own management in 1901, with Matheson Lang, and later Harcourt Williams, as Benedick. But subsequent revivals, during the succeeding forty years or so, were not greatly successful, and playgoers and critics too young to remember Ellen Terry seemed to find the play ill-balanced and even tedious and unconvincing. Irving's production, of course, was lavish, realistic, and drastically pruned of the many improper allusions with which the comedy abounds. Sir Johnston Forbes-Robertson (who played Claudio at the Lyceum, and was to challenge his old master, Irving, a few years later as the great Hamlet of his generation) was a painter as well as an actor in his earlier years, and his picture of the church scene, as he appeared in it with Irving and Ellen Terry, has often been reproduced. From this we can see how the scene was staged and costumed, and can imagine how impressive it must have seemed to the delighted audiences of the eighteen-eighties.

Benedick and Beatrice are the heart of the play, and leading players acting these parts have naturally made the most of their opportunities. But, as was the fashion until the advent of the cinema, the leading characters in Shakespeare were often played by actors who were really far too old, and the rest of the cast had to be balanced accordingly. This compromise can be especially dangerous in *Much Ado*. Unless Beatrice is acted by quite a young woman, her passionate championing of Hero and her diatribes against marriage lose half their point. Don Pedro, Benedick and Don John must be eligible young bachelors, Pedro, perhaps, a little older than the other two, and Claudio and Hero as young as possible: two attractive children, with all the impetuosity and inexperience that may excuse the highly improbable development of their love-story, on which the rather awkward plot depends.

The play demands high spirits, dash and style. Most of the wit verges on sexual innuendo, and is only amusing when uttered with directness and a spontaneous sense of fun. We accept the implausible Don John and his villainy (surely a first sketch for Iago?), the tantrums of Claudio, and the illogical credulity of the Prince; and, while we are watching the play, we shall scarcely notice that Margaret does not go to the wedding, though her absence is unexplained and extremely unlikely. One word from her, of course, and there would be no fourth and fifth acts. So Shakespeare conveniently forgets her, and also carefully avoids showing us the scene when she talks to Borachio out of Hero's chamber-window – for this would have been visually too important, and the audience would have challenged its veracity.[1]

The splendour and variety of the church scene sweeps away

---

[1] I once saw a production at Stratford which interpolated this very episode in dumb show – disastrously for the play, in my opinion.

our demand for logic, as we listen to Claudio's outburst, Leonato's fine denunciation, and the great serio-comic scene between Beatrice and Benedick, which carries us forward to Benedick's challenge, the unravelling of the plot, and the inevitable happy ending. We may find it hard to forgive the Prince and Claudio. We may think Hero a goose for not speaking up, and Margaret a ninny for allowing herself to be made a party to the deception. But these are minor blemishes, born of our modern way of thinking. The plot is lively and varied, the prose superb in cadence, rhythm, and humour, the verse scenes charmingly disposed with a lyric lightness.

The ingenious setting which was used in my production of *Much Ado About Nothing* was evolved in a curious way. In 1936 I had seen, at the old Alhambra in London, a ballet of *Don Juan* by Michael Fokine with music by Gluck. I made a note of the artist who had designed the striking scenery and costumes, and found that he was a Spaniard living in France; and some years after, during the war, when I was to direct Sierra's *The Cradle Song*, I tried to find out his address, but was told by the Leicester Galleries, to whom I applied, that they did not know what had become of him. In 1948 I visited Paris for a weekend to see some plays, one of which, *Le Maître de Santiago*, I had been told would interest me. The leading actor was ill and there was no performance, but on the bill, in the lobby of the hotel, I saw, as the designer of the scenery, the name of Mariano Andreu, the Spanish artist I had been seeking for so many years. Soon after this I was approached by Anthony Quayle to direct *Much Ado About Nothing*, and he, on my suggestion, sought out Andreu in Paris and persuaded him to come to Stratford-on-Avon to design it.

M. Andreu has very little English, and my French is elementary, so our early talks proceeded in a somewhat disjointed way, with many gaps and misunderstandings. And yet we seemed to understand each other immediately. I told him I had always imagined *Much Ado* with scenery and dresses of the Boccaccio period, the action taking place, perhaps, on a terrace above the city, out of doors, where all the dancing and intrigue would seem romantically lively. I also suggested two small temples which might stand on the stage throughout, to be used as arbours in the two over-hearing scenes in Leonato's garden, and I thought perhaps that these should be made to revolve so as to be used also for the entrance to the church, for I had an idea that it might be simpler and more effective to play the so-called 'Church Scene' out of doors, the Friar meeting the bride and bridegroom at the doors. This would obviate the complications of a realistic church interior, which had always seemed to me too naturalistic to fit the romantic fantasy of my imagination.

When, in other productions of the play that I had seen, the actors were encumbered with Elizabethan dress – farthingales, ruffs and trunk hose – I had always felt that these costumes, always difficult for modern actors to wear, seemed to make the play heavy and over-realistic. Andreu listened attentively, and I wondered how much of my headlong chatter he had understood. The designs he sent me a few weeks later were generously influenced by many of my ideas, and yet the artist's own contribution was entirely original. He gave me my garden, but varied it ingeniously so that it could be opened on hinges by attendants, and the screen walls thus became an unrealistic interior, with the trees of the garden and the sky still showing over the top. The stage space was quite uncluttered by the scenery, and there were many angled entrances and exits (most necessary in this play, to give a constant movement and gaiety of speed). The beautiful costume designs were inspired by

Pisanello and Piero della Francesca, but somewhat fantasticated in Andreu's own original style.

The designer had several other delightful surprises for me. One day, when we were looking at some books together in my house, we saw a design for Otway's *Venice Preserv'd* in Gordon Craig's *Towards a New Theatre*. I passed it to Andreu and said, 'How lovely this would be on the stage, a balcony over a colonnade of pillars.' He gave one look at the drawing and said, 'It would be splendid to build a front scene like this solidly, on two levels.' I began to work with him on this idea, and thought of showing Benedick shaving on the upper stage in the scene which follows his hiding in the arbour when his friends convince him that Beatrice is in love with him. As a pendant, I evolved a similar arrangement for a later scene – Beatrice standing below, while Hero and Margaret, dressing for the wedding on the balcony above, mock her about her new-found love for Benedick. These two episodes could thus be acted with a varied use of the stage space, while a second more spacious street scene could be set ready behind the colonnade. In this wider area the scene of the watch took place – while the penthouse in the centre at the back was finally opened like a Chinese box by the pages and became the interior of the church. Though it was easy with the garden and street scenes of the first act to let the pages enter to open and close the scenery with music playing, while the lighting slowly changed and the audience looked on, Andreu did not wish to repeat this effect all through the evening, and yet it seemed impossible to strike the front colonnade, with its solid floor and practical balcony above, without an interval, a black-out, or the dropping of the house curtain.

After many frenzied discussions in pidgin French and English, Andreu conceived the idea of a bridge – a *passerelle* he called it. This word, unknown to us before, became a kind of grim joke, during our conferences, as being the principal obstacle to the smoothness of our carefully timed production. None of the technical staff thought the *passerelle* could be made to work, for, in order to make the balconies slide away, one to each side, there had to be some contrivance by which the central bridge would open of itself. Everybody said this was impossible. But, to our intense satisfaction, the head carpenter at Stratford, not so easily balked, evolved two sliding platforms on the principle of a matchbox, and, lo and behold, they slid away as smoothly as butter when pulled from behind the wings on each side, and the scene was changed in a twinkling. It was exciting to see how a front scene, built solidly, and sliding away from left and right, with a small backcloth above rising at the same time, gave a certain pictorial grace and novelty to the changing of the scene, and the effect was thus far less disturbing to the flow of the action than the usual raising of a plain front cloth or the time-worn cliché of opening runner curtains.

I was glad, in this production, to be able to prove one of my favourite theories; that, in the over-hearing scenes in Shakespeare, the character at whom the scene is aimed should be closest to the audience. In *Twelfth Night*, on the other hand, the famous scene of Malvolio with the letter should, in my opinion, be acted the other way round – that is, with the plotters on the fore-stage, and Malvolio further from the audience, for I feel sure that the Elizabethan comedians, making their jokes at Malvolio's expense while he is reading the letter, must have tossed their remarks over their shoulders to the groundlings standing close to them on the apron, almost in the position of eavesdroppers themselves.[1]

---

[1] In an admirable production of *Twelfth Night* in Paris (with Suzanne Flon doubling the parts of Viola and Sebastian in a prose translation by Jean Anouilh) I was especially delighted with the direction of the Letter Scene. The plotters, beginning on the fore-stage, concealed themselves

In Shakespeare directors often have a tendency to make things easier for an actor delivering a long, and perhaps wordy, speech by making the other characters interrupt at intervals with gestures, movements, changing of positions, and even spoken exclamations, but this is surely a cheap device. It is also, I think, a mistake for the director to display too many ingenuities of grouping and pageantry, if important characters are ill-positioned in consequence so that important passages become inaudible or blurred. It is vital for the characters to be close together or far apart according to the way the dialogue may most effectively be thrown from one to the other. And it is of course immensely important also to decide beforehand the exact placing of the furniture on the stage, especially as with a permanent setting it will probably have to remain there for a great number of scenes – perhaps throughout the whole evening. Thus, in *Much Ado*, I simplified the action by having two angled benches in the first act which were never moved, except for a moment in the dance scene, after which the pages put them back again. In the second part we had a completely bare stage (though there were stools in the balcony, and below in the colonnade), and in the last section of the play a pedestal on which characters could stand or sit. This directed most of the action naturally towards the centre of the stage, and the block could also be used for a table in the scene of Dogberry's examination.

Much Ado, it seems to me, is above all a play of the Renaissance.

---

behind little flowering shrubs in pots, and followed Malvolio round the stage. Thus he was able to speak much of his soliloquy at the front, and then moved on, while the listeners took his place to confide their asides to the audience. Malvolio occasionally glanced at the shrubs over his shoulder, wondering whether they were not perhaps in a different place from usual! This was a most amusing device, and the director arranged it brilliantly. He also made a splendidly convincing character of Malvolio and was one of the best I have ever seen.

It may conceivably be played in a décor of an earlier period than Shakespeare's. But I have been amazed, in the last few years, to find it, both at Stratford-on-Avon, the Old Vic, Stratford Ontario, and Stratford Connecticut, decked out in Victorian or Regency scenery and costumes, without much protest from audiences or critics. Surely the period between 1800 and 1900, when women barely showed their ankles, and conversation between the sexes was intensely prudish and reserved, is in direct contradiction of Shakespeare's whole intention in the text.

I have only lately come to realize that the great classic writers have so often founded their comedies on the difference between reality and sham. In *The Merchant of Venice*, *Twelfth Night*, *Measure For Measure*, and *Much Ado About Nothing*, the same point is made again and again. In *As You Like It* Shakespeare continually emphasizes the contrast between court and country life. Similarly in the later comedies, *The Winter's Tale*, *Cymbeline*, and *The Tempest*, the shallow cruelties and false values of society are contrasted against the innocence of youth, the honesty of simple folk. The wonder of journeys and shipwrecks, strange restorings of lost dear ones, are also used to evoke scenes of magical atmosphere: the mountain caves of Wales, the sheep-shearing festival, the thunder and lightning, as the Oracle from Delphi is read out at Hermione's trial, and the smashing of timbers and crash of waves as Alonso's ship goes down on the shores of Prospero's magic island.

The idea of choosing *The Winter's Tale* for a Festival production, in the year 1951, suggested itself to me largely because of the success of *Measure For Measure* at Stratford-on-Avon the year before, when the audiences had seemed to find so much interest in one of the lesser-known plays, and I had had the exciting experience of working with Peter Brook as Director for the first time.

I had seen *The Winter's Tale* several times at the Old Vic and Stratford, and though greatly struck by the beauty of many of its scenes, I thought there was a good deal in it that seemed obscure, and a diversity of action that was difficult to integrate. However, I realized at once that the plot is full of effective theatrical surprises (like *Measure For Measure*).

Familiarity with the more hackneyed plays has destroyed this sense of surprise to a very large extent for the average modern audience, yet, however fantastic the stories may seem when examined coldly, they are always capable of holding an audience in the theatre if they are imaginatively staged, even though, in order to enjoy *Measure For Measure* and *The Winter's Tale*, one must suspend logical belief and accept the plays as a mixture of fairy tale and mystery.

Similarly with the characters. Neither Angelo nor Leontes is a wholly realistic figure, though one is a narrow, priggish hypocrite and the other a jealous tyrant. Both are presented in comparatively few scenes, and therefore not elaborated with the same detail as the protagonists of the great tragic plays. The characters are somewhat stylized, symbolic, and tremendously concentrated. We are shown in one, almost without preparation, the hideous secret lust of Angelo, and in the other the violent unreasoning hysteria of Leontes. But it is no use trying to act these parts if one imagines them to be melodramatic monsters without a shred of humanity. We have all felt jealousy and lust in some form or another. They are two of the most human failings of mankind. In excess they almost become diseases, and they can easily grow into obsessions.

I have never played Iago, who is, with Richard the Third, one of the few Shakespeare characters to boast openly of his evil – but he must, I think, if an actor is to play him convincingly, justify his wickedness to himself. A really evil person must be without moral sense – and Iago (like Duke Ferdinand in *The Duchess of Malfi*, a part I once acted without much pleasure) is really a monster. Angelo and Leontes, on the other hand, are both given wonderful scenes of repentance, in which they are shamed, humiliated, and at last forgiven. These later scenes give a fine opportunity for the actor to show both sides of the characters, and, though the scenes themselves are very short (Angelo has only one or two speeches in a long scene of silence), they are extraordinarily vivid and telling. Shylock, of course, is shamed and humiliated too, but hardly forgiven.

No one but Shakespeare would have known how to move generations of playgoers with the final scenes of Macbeth and Shylock, both of whom are greater sinners even than Angelo and Leontes. The main difficulty with the two latter characters is that their violent actions are liable to appear unreasonably sudden, and consequently more difficult to make convincing to a modern audience. But if the actor believes in them sincerely as human beings, their behaviour may be made to seem dramatic, and even logical, within the framework of fantasy with which Shakespeare has carefully surrounded them.

Until I acted Leontes, and Cassius in *Julius Caesar*, I had never imagined I could convince an audience in the part of a jealous man. Jealousy is a weakness that I do not suffer from in any marked degree, though I cannot pretend that I have not occasionally, both in my private and professional life, known something of the indignities of that emotion.

Leontes' jealousy is something of a fantasy, born of his own imagination; that of Cassius an innate sense of frustrated power, which he longs to use in order to dominate Brutus and revenge himself on Caesar, while Iago and Richard the Third have a baleful, deep-seated malevolence which colours their entire behaviour and personality. Both these men are cold and insensitive, whereas Cassius is passionate and febrile. But Cassius, though frustrated and bitter, is a practical man of action, whereas Leontes is a highly imaginative, poetical tyrant, a megalomaniac. In contrast to these three extraordinary studies of jealous men (Leontes, Cassius and Iago) Shakespeare has also drawn the marvellous character of Othello, a man 'not easily jealous, but ... perplex'd in the extreme' – a part more fascinating, to me at any rate, than either Cassius or Leontes, though in attempting it I foolishly imagined that the character, being more basically sympathetic and more fully drawn than the other two, would be easier to bring to life. I was soon to discover that I was mistaken.

After acting Cassius at Stratford on the stage in the 1950 season, I played the same part again for M.G.M. in Hollywood, in 1952, in the film of *Julius Caesar*. I had always been somewhat sceptical as to the artistic merit of presenting Shakespeare's plays in another medium, whether radio, television or the cinema, although I found the film of *Henry V* a remarkable achievement.

Julius Caesar, like *Henry V*, is a familiar and straightforward play, though the division of sympathy between the characters of Cassius, Antony and Brutus has always made it difficult to cast in the theatre with perfect balance. In the theatre, too, the battle scenes, written and constructed in the conventional Elizabethan pattern, are difficult to present convincingly, and are apt to give a sense of disappointment and anti-climax after the power and variety of the first three acts. The same fault was, strangely enough, equally evident in the film version, in spite of the wider range and greater resources of the screen.

There was a famous production of *Julius Caesar* by Sir Herbert Tree at His Majesty's Theatre in London in the early nineteen hundreds. The highly realistic décor was designed by Alma-Tadema, then a fashionable Academic painter. The crowd scenes, inspired by the Meiningen Company of Germany (which had visited London some years before) were considered a miracle of verisimilitude and stage management. In those days supers and stage hands were comparatively inexpensive, and professional soldiers could supplement their weekly pay by 'walking on', for a few shillings a night, to give an authentically military air to the Roman Legions. Three leading actors strove to outshine one another in the roles of Antony, Brutus and Cassius – Herbert Tree (Antony), Lewis Waller (Brutus), and Franklin McLeay (Cassius). The part of Antony was always considered the prerogative of the Actor-Manager; in America, some years before, the three great Booth brothers had made an appearance in the play together, and had even alternated parts at different performances.

In our day, however, *Caesar* has not been so often revived in the theatre either in London or New York, though Orson Welles's New York production in Fascist dress in 1937 was much praised and is still remembered. Henry Ainley acted the part of Antony at the St James's Theatre in London during his management there, soon after the first world war, but the production did not meet with any great success.

There are of course many fine stage directors who could be trusted to direct the crowd scenes in the theatre with great effect. But these scenes, important though they are, cannot, however ably stage-managed, carry the whole tragedy to success; and a simpler method of presentation, stripped to essentials with a small company, such as would be economically more practical in our theatre today, would, I think, hardly lend itself very happily to this particular play.

At Stratford-on-Avon, when I played Cassius there in 1950 (under the direction of Anthony Quayle and Michael Langham), the production seemed to be greatly enjoyed by the public, but the actors were not so happy. Although I learnt much about the part of Cassius which stood me in good stead when I came to appear in the film two years later, I never looked forward to *Caesar* nights at Stratford. The verse pitched, almost throughout, in a lofty, rhetorical style, is very tiring and difficult for the actors to sustain without monotony in a large theatre. There is little prose to vary it, and it is difficult for the leading characters to keep continuously alive against the mass of restless citizens, senators, and soldiers who must continually revolve and shout around them. There is little feminine interest to give the play domestic warmth and relaxation. The classical costumes, though becoming and graceful to players of fine physique, can be ridiculous and hampering to men who are too short, too tall, too thin or too fat. There is always a danger of the effect of a lot of gentlemen sitting on marble benches in a Turkish bath. There may be something to be said for experimenting with a production in Elizabethan dress, and yet it might only be confusing to see a Brutus looking like Guy Fawkes, or a Caesar crowned with laurel, wearing a beard and dressed in doublet and hose, thus adding further anachronisms to those which Shakespeare has already provided in his text. Unlocalized scenery – balconies, rostrums, and bare boards – may serve well enough for Roman streets, the Forum and the senate-house, but they will hardly serve to conjure up Brutus's orchard, his tent, and Philippi fields, even though Shakespeare's audiences may have found no difficulty in so imagining them on the open stage of the Globe three hundred years ago. The play bristles with hazards of all kinds both for actors and directors, even on the stage.

When I first read the script of the *Caesar* film, I was immediately impressed by the faithful way in which the text had been respected and adapted for the screen. Of course it is impossible to film Shakespeare in complete accordance with the text – but naturally the less the sequence of scenes is tampered with, the nearer one may hope for the cumulative effect which Shakespeare himself intended. The more I studied the film version, the better it seemed to me to have been planned, both as a cut version of the play and as a scenario for the screen. I felt, as never before, that here was one of the few Shakespearian plays which *might* be more satisfactory in the cinema than it ever can be in the theatre, save under most exceptional circumstances. The short talk I had with the director of the film, Joseph Mankiewicz, when he first approached me in London and told me some of his ideas, confirmed my enthusiasm for the experiment.

In the screen version there are hardly any major omissions. The short scene with Portia, Lucius and Soothsayer is cut – a daring loss, since it makes the lack of female interest still more marked. Gone, too, is the lynching of Cinna the Poet. (Actually this scene was shot for the film version, but it disappeared in the cutting-room – no doubt owing to its irrelevance to the main story and the necessity to shorten the playing time and preserve continuity as far as possible.)

I found that the producer,[1] John Houseman, and Mr Mankiewicz had used the technique of the screen to the utmost advantage in devising close-ups, and also in many details illustrating key moments in film terms – (the blind Soothsayer with his staff of jingling bells, rising slowly from the steps where he sits half hidden by the crowd – Casca's sweating forehead as he moves through the crowd of conspirators to strike the first blow at Caesar) – and, above all, in the striking contrasts of close-ups, distances, and angles. Shakespeare himself would surely have been pleased to be able to transport his audience in a few seconds from the hot sunlight of the stadium, where Caesar

---

[1] In film parlance 'producer' is an overall supervisor, 'director' the man who actually directs the scenes as they are shot.

passes Brutus, Cassius and Casca on his return from the games with Antony, to the night scene with its flapping shutters and slippery cobblestones where Cicero hurries by and Cassius and Casca whisper as they meet to plan Caesar's murder. And then, a moment later, the camera slides on again to the silent garden, where Brutus paces to and fro, in troubled indecision, amid the shattered branches and litter of the storm.

The elaborate scenic backgrounds, the milling crowds, filling the screen at one moment or receding at will to a respectful distance, allow the main characters to fill the foreground, dominating Rome and its unruly citizens with ease. We can follow every character's reactions in detail, both in speech and expression. Gesticulation and shouting – both of which are necessary in the theatre in so many scenes of this play – can be reduced to a minimum on the screen, where every look, every subtlety of phrasing, can be caught by the camera in a flash. The scenes can progress with apparent reality and speed, rather than in the heavy theatrical 'classical' manner, which can so easily make Cassius a ranter and Brutus a pompous prig. Thunder, the din of battle, and the shouting of the vociferous throng can be timed and modulated so as to allow every line of dialogue to be easily heard. And, since there are few philosophical passages (and only two short soliloquies) in this play, the difficulty of transmitting an abstract poetic mood, such as is necessary in the more imaginative plays of Shakespeare, does not arise. The film, I think, gives a real and rare feeling that the verse medium might be natural to the speakers, and it may be that future experiments with Shakespeare on the screen may show even more striking possibilities of imagery and vocal subtleties.

5

GRANVILLE-BARKER REHEARSES
KING LEAR

IN THE ILL-FATED SPRING of 1940, just before the Fall of France, Granville-Barker accepted an invitation from Tyrone Guthrie and myself to direct a production of *King Lear* at the Old Vic. The company assembled was a fine one, including as it did Jack Hawkins, Jessica Tandy, Robert Harris, Fay Compton, Cathleen Nesbitt, Lewis Casson, Nicholas Hannen, Stephen Haggard and Harcourt Williams.

Granville-Barker came over from Paris, and spent a week-end making preliminary arrangements with Roger Furse, the designer, and with Lewis Casson, who agreed to undertake the preparatory work of the production. Barker refused to have his name officially announced as director, and only agreed to supervise some rehearsals, using his own preface to the play as a foundation. I went to see him at the Queen's Theatre, and nervously endeavoured to read the part through with him. When I got to the end he remarked: 'You got two lines right. Now we will begin to work.' He also said: 'Lear is an oak. You are an ash. We must see how this will serve you.' I left him, deeply apprehensive of my limitations, but with my copy of the text thick with brilliantly suggestive notes.[1]

He came back to London again after rehearsals had already begun and worked with the actors for ten days, but he left after

[1] See Appendix 1

E

the first dress-rehearsal, and never saw a performance with an audience.

I have often been surprised to find that a very fine theatrical talent does not seem to become rusty through a long period of disuse. It has been suggested that the brilliance of Ellen Terry's work in her middle years may have been deepened and enriched, after her rigorous training as a child actress, by the six years in which she left the theatre and lived privately bringing up her children in the country. Harley Granville-Barker, when I first knew him in the thirties, had not worked professionally in the theatre for twenty years, but he showed no signs, as he resumed work with a company almost completely unknown to him, of any old-fashioned narrowness of outlook or loss of sensitivity. In the very few days in which I had the privilege of working with him, I could see no trace of effort in the use of his superlative gifts – no lack of sureness in his authority, no hint of tentativeness or uncertainty in his approach. From the moment he stepped through the stage-door at the Old Vic, he inspired and dominated everyone like a master-craftsman, and everyone in the theatre recognized this at once.

He had only ten days to work with us on *King Lear*, but they were the fullest in experience that I have ever had in all my years upon the stage. By letter, and at some early conferences, he had already devised a ground-plan for the production, simple patterns of levels and entrances, diagrams showing how the furniture should be placed, and so on. In all these matters he had shown a masterly understanding of the scenic essentials that he felt to be demanded by the text. A few weeks later, when rehearsals had already been held under Lewis Casson and Tyrone Guthrie for some days, he arrived and began to work with the actors, not using any notes, but sitting on the stage with his back to the footlights, a copy of the play in his hand, tortoise-shell spectacles well forward on his nose, dressed in a black business suit, his bushy red eyebrows jutting forward, quiet-voiced, seldom moving, coldly humorous, shrewdly observant, infinitely patient and persevering.

Although he had a very strong conception of how every character should be played, he did not at first try to force his views upon the actors or attempt to discourage their ideas, though he frequently corrected them. He was, as he told me, a great believer in reading the play round a table for a week or more, but on this occasion there was no time for that. His first concern was certainly for the speaking of the verse and the balance of the voices. In dealing with the actors he was quite impersonal, calling everyone by the name of the part they were playing. He neither coaxed nor flattered, but at the same time, though he was intensely autocratic and severe, he was never personal or rude. The actors had immediate respect for his authority. They did not become paralysed or apathetic, as can so often happen when a strong director is not excessively sensitive. They were constantly dismayed, however, by the high standards he continually demanded of them, and by the intense hard work to which he subjected them without showing any appearance of fatigue himself. For, the moment they appeared to begin to satisfy him in one direction, Barker was urging them on to experiment in another. Tempo, atmosphere, diction, balance, character – no detail could escape his fastidious ear, his unerring dramatic instinct and his superb sense of classic shapeliness of line.

And yet he was in no way old-fashioned. He was not afraid to have an actor standing downstage or with his back to the audience. On the other hand, he had none of the modern fear of clichés in the acting of Shakespeare – what is called 'ham acting' when it is crudely executed. He encouraged grand entrances and exits centre-stage, a declamatory style, imposing gestures. Only under his subtle hand these theatrical devices became classic, tragic, noble, not merely histrionic or melodramatic, because of the unerring taste and simplicity with which he ordered them.

To my great regret, I never saw him handle supers or drill a crowd scene; indeed, to those of us in the company who had hung on his every word during those short ten days, it seemed something of a disaster that he did not feel free to stay and guide us to the end, either to final victory or defeat. I suppose he was no longer prepared to face the tedious anxieties of the last days before production – the lighting plots, music cues and last-minute adjustments and emergencies, the publicity, photographs and gossip. I think he had ceased to care about the reactions of audiences or the opinions of dramatic critics. The actual working life of the theatre with its petty involvements no longer concerned him. Certainly, he was himself the finest audience and severest critic I have ever set myself to try and please. Praise from him was praise worth waiting for, but it was rare, and often rather implied than stated. 'You did some fine things today in that scene' he would say to me, 'I hope you know what they were!' and then proceed to read me a long list of my mistakes.

Barker left us to return to Paris, and the production opened without him. Yet for several weeks afterwards I kept receiving postcards and short notes from him, indicating improvements and suggesting details, showing that his mind was not entirely free of his work with us, and that it had even moved him to a reconsidered study of the play.[1]

Incidentally, in the few glimpses which he gave us at rehearsal, he must have been a very fine actor himself, with extraordinary power and repose, though no great range of voice. Of his supremacy as a director no one who had the good fortune

[1] See Appendix 1

to attend those rehearsals can have any possible doubt.

But he loved writing more than the theatre, and Shakespeare perhaps better than either. At least we have the *Prefaces* to comfort us, in some degree at least, for the great man we have lost. He gave so much of his fine early work to the English theatre that one cannot help regretting all it might perhaps have gained over his later years, if only he could have been persuaded to continue working there.

6

A NOTE ON HAMLET

To PLAY THE PART of Hamlet is the ambition of every young actor. I played it first at the Old Vic and Queen's Theatres in London in 1929 at the age of 25, and since then I have appeared in four subsequent revivals, in 1934 in London, 1936 in New York, 1939 (London and Kronborg Castle, Elsinore), and finally in London in 1944. Thus I have studied and experimented with the role for over fifteen years of my life of fifty-nine years.

How old is Hamlet according to the text? At the opening of the play he thinks of returning to school at Wittenberg, and in the last act the Gravedigger says that he is exactly thirty years of age. Does Shakespeare imply a passage of some considerable time during the course of the play, as he seems to do also in *Macbeth*? I think he does.

In any event Hamlet must be a young man, though probably not an adolescent. And his mother must seem to be a woman of young middle age, for a Gertrude older than 50 must surely be unconvincing on the stage.

I was fortunate in being one of the first actors, I believe, in England (except for Master Betty – the child prodigy who had a short but spectacular success in London in the early nineteenth century) to have the opportunity of playing the part of Hamlet before I was thirty. My youthful appearance certainly told in my favour with the public, who had, over many years, been accustomed to expect in Hamlet an older, more established star. My first Hamlet was probably somewhat hysterical. The angry young man of the twenties was somewhat more decadent (and rather more affected it now seems to me) than his counterpart in the fifties and sixties, but the rebellion against convention, the violence and bitterness, has surely always been the same in every generation.

The part demands declamation, macabre humour, passionate violence, philosophical reflection. There are scenes of love and tenderness, outbursts of bitterness and despair. It is a temptation for the actor to develop the possibilities of each scene for its individual histrionic effect, instead of presenting a complete basic character in which the part may progress in a simple convincing line. Hamlet must seem to experience before the audience everything that happens to him in the course of the play, and the actor must find in himself his own sincerest personal reactions to every episode – grief at his father's death, disillusionment with his mother and Ophelia, horror and anguish with the Ghost, and so on. The scenes themselves are so strikingly dramatic that they may betray the actor into sheer effectiveness (in a theatrical sense), more easily attained than the truth that will reveal the man himself. It was only as I grew older and more experienced that I became aware of these pitfalls (after I had worked with two or three different talented directors, and when, in two different productions, I directed the play myself as well as acting in it), though I tried continually to find a way to simplify, to use the verse and prose to express the variety of emotions conveyed so wonderfully in the text, and to balance the neurotic youthful side of the part by adding to it maturer qualities of strength, manliness and wit.

Hamlet is the many-sided, many-talented Elizabethan man – prince, son, courtier, swordsman, philosopher, lover, friend. In the Renaissance world a gifted, vital man crammed into fifty years all the variety of experience that may be spread over eighty years of life today. In the exquisite character of Hamlet, there is a richness of expression, a delicate perceptivity, a general curiosity; he has distinctive grace and breeding, which never degenerates into snobbery or decadence. The other principal characters, Claudius, Polonius, Laertes, Osric, Rosencrantz and Guildenstern, the foolish Ophelia, the sensual Gertrude – are shifting, worldly creatures drawn in deliberate contrast to the finer natures in the play – the forthright, sensitive Hamlet, the agonized, wronged Ghost, the steadfast, devoted Horatio, and the simple honest men, the First Player and the Gravedigger. These last three characters are the only men in the play with whom Hamlet can talk with the ease and directness which he so longs for in the world of disillusion which surrounds him.

Fortinbras, his *alter ego*, whom he never meets, only pervades the tragedy by hearsay, until, after once passing across the stage half-way through the action, he enters magnificently in the last scene to speak the valedictory lines on a rising note of hope.

It is sometimes lucky for an actor to tackle a great role for the first time before he is fully aware of its difficulties. I acted Macbeth (and King Lear too) before I was thirty, and, even with these dark, mature, heroic figures, I was more successful, I think, in giving a broad sketch of the characters when I attempted them with an almost naïve approach, than in subsequent productions in which I had had time to realize the enormously difficult intellectual and technical problems involved. With Hamlet it was the same, though of course long practice and experiment gave my acting in that part more assurance and skill as the years went by. On the other hand I became in the end somewhat confused in some of my decisions on readings, business, and so on, through being too ready to listen to the opinions of critics, directors and members of the audience, some of whose suggestions were of course invaluable, but whose inconsistencies tended to confuse my imagination so that I feared to lose the essential basis of my original conception.

In spite of all its complicated problems of psychology, I believe Hamlet is what we actors call a 'straight' part. The man who essays it must obviously be equipped with certain essential qualities – grace of person and princely bearing, youth, energy, humour and sensitivity. He must have a pleasing voice of great range, and a meticulous ear for verse and prose. He must be neither slow nor ponderous. He must have wit and gentleness, but also power, edge, and a sense of the macabre. He must fascinate by his quick changes of mood. The soliloquies and cadenzas must be spoken in a special way to distinguish them from the conversational scenes, but without losing either humanity, rhythm, pace, or urgency. Hamlet must impress us with his loneliness and agonies of soul without seeming portentous or self-pitying. He must thrill us when he sees the Ghost, drives Claudius from the Gonzago play, stabs Polonius, reveals himself at the graveside, and throws himself upon Laertes. In no other part that I have played have I found it so difficult to know whether I became Hamlet or Hamlet became me, for the association of an actor with such a character is an extraordinarily subtle transformation, an almost indefinable mixture of imagination and impersonation.

In the theatre, of course, where luck plays so great a part (but not quite as great, I think, as some people are inclined to suppose), I was particularly lucky to have the opportunities which gave me the chance I needed. I played Hamlet as I imagined him, using many of my own ideas, and helped by the directors and actors I had the good fortune to work with in the various revivals in which I appeared. Hamlet, it seems to me, must be re-discovered, re-created, every ten or fifteen years. The changes in the world must affect the directors and actors who seek to create him, as well as the reactions of the audiences.

The problems of Hamlet can never be completely solved for the actor. It is a part of unexampled difficulty and, though it provides such a variety of range that no good actor can really fail in it entirely (for he is bound to succeed in certain scenes), the demands of the character are so tremendous that one feels no actor should be asked to play it more than once or twice a week. For in such a part the player must really live and die before our eyes.

7

HERITAGE FROM HAMMERSMITH

SIR NIGEL PLAYFAIR was largely responsible for the interest and popularity in London, during the twenties, of eighteenth-century plays and operas. His own personal taste and enthusiasm were matched by the genius of his friend Claude Lovat Fraser, whose early death, in 1922, robbed the English theatre of one of its outstanding talents. Directors are sometimes criticized for their loyalty to individual designers, but those of us who have worked over many years in the theatre know how valuable it is to plan a production with a collaborator who is familiar with our particular methods, and who can contribute constructively in exchanging views about the approach to and handling of a play. I worked in this way with the firm of Motley (three talented women, Peggy and Sophia Harris, and Elizabeth Montgomery) from 1932 to 1938, with ever-increasing confidence and a considerable measure of success. In the same way Basil Dean collaborated for many years with George Harris (whom he had met in Liverpool) as his designer, until the latter's death; Tyrone Guthrie, over a great number of years, had been equally successful working with Tanya Moiseiwitsch, who has brilliantly designed so many of his productions.

Lovat Fraser's stylized décor for *As You Like It* at the Lyric Hammersmith for Playfair in 1919 caused generally adverse comment. It was before its time, breaking new ground, just as Norman Wilkinson's gold fairies and green curtains for *A Midsummer Night's Dream* and Albert Rutherston's stylized *Winter's Tale* and *Twelfth Night* had done when the public was scared and shocked by their innovations during Barker's seasons at the Savoy before the first world war. It was not until the famous Playfair production of *The Beggar's Opera* in 1920 that Lovat Fraser's simple permanent setting and bright simplified costumes suddenly became the rage. Playfair's whole production was original, pretty, and elegant, with just enough wit and bite to prevent it from becoming sentimental. The company, with the exception of Frederick Ranalow and Sylvia Nelis (both recruited from Sir Thomas Beecham's Opera Company) were little known, but admirably chosen and rehearsed, and the opera ran for several years on end, while the inevitable changes in the cast during that time did nothing to lessen its popularity. Then, with the death of Lovat Fraser, Playfair was forced to find other collaborators.

In 1924, Playfair announced *The Way of the World*[1] by Congreve for the Lyric Hammersmith, and the décor for this revival was entrusted to Doris Zinkeisen, whose painted scenery and vivid costumes, in poster style, more elaborate but less fastidious than the work of Lovat Fraser, were, to the eyes of the playgoers of the twenties, distinctly *avant-garde*. But it was, above all, the acting of Edith Evans as Millamant and Robert Loraine as Mirabel which brought the public to see the revival of a classic which no one had imagined could possibly succeed with a modern audience. Playfair's direction, despite several weaknesses in the supporting cast, showed the same skill in simplification that he had already achieved in *The Beggar's Opera*. *The Way of the World* (as I realized more fully when I came to direct the play myself in 1953, also at the Lyric Hammersmith) has an impossibly difficult plot line, and cutting and transposition seem to be of little use in making its complications easier to follow. But it is full of brilliant virtuoso scenes and superbly drawn characters, though Millamant is too often absent from the stage.

Love for Love[1] is much more lucid, though here too the dramatic action is of comparatively little importance. Everything depends, in both plays, on the ability of the performers to present rich human types, and to deliver the elaborate speeches with sufficient relish and wit to re-create the leisured but robust style of Congreve's age and metaphor.

We know, from contemporary prints and pictures, how the comedies must have been originally staged – the two proscenium doors opening on to the fore-stage on either side of the curtain (as they still remain at the beautiful little Theatre Royal, Bristol), the painted drop scenes, open wings, the candles in chandeliers and footlights, and the formal, simplified arrangement of the few pieces of furniture. Presumably the lighting was not changed throughout the performance, except when the servants came on and off to snuff the candles or replace them when they had burnt out. This may be partly the reason why Congreve (like Sheridan) does not seem to trouble with meticulous indications of scenes and times of day. In *The Way of the World* the action begins in a Coffee House and then moves to an outdoor scene in St James's Park. After this, the action takes place entirely in Lady Wishfort's house, her dressing-room, and some larger reception room; while in *Love for Love*, the action alternates between Valentine's lodgings and Foresight's house. Today, when there must not be more than two intervals in the theatre, it is necessary to devise quick changes, and not to confuse the audience (or increase the expense) by having too many changes of scenes and costumes. Playfair always contrived in his productions to give a decorative, pleasing series of pictures without

[1] See Appendix 3

undue elaboration. This was partly imposed on him by the fact that he worked in such a small theatre with a very low budget. But he was also resolved to abolish the traditions of the Victorian and Edwardian productions of eighteenth-century plays which had so often been cut, bowdlerized, and cluttered with elaborately built scenery, long intervals, pages, minuets, and animals. These picturesque *divertissements* were sure to please those theatre-goers who might otherwise be too bored to listen to long speeches, classical allusions, and complicated dialogue.

The characters in Congreve seem somewhat larger than life, those in Sheridan more human, warm, and nearer to our own age, while Goldsmith's are positively domesticated. Each author requires a different style of acting and direction. Edith Evans's performance as Millamant was probably the finest stylized piece of bravura acting seen in London in the last fifty years. Her economy and grace of movement, her perfectly sustained poses, the purring coquetry of her voice with its extraordinary subtlety of range, was inimitably captivating. Like her definitive Nurse in *Romeo and Juliet*, her inspired Rosalind, and her famous Lady Bracknell, she presented, in each case, a complete universal type as well as an individual woman. Playfair subsequently revived *The Old Bachelor* of Congreve for her, but her part was small and did not allow her sufficient scope for her talents, though later, in *The Beaux' Stratagem* of Farquhar, she gave another fine performance under his direction.

Playfair presented several other eighteenth-century plays and operas: *Love In A Village*, *The Rivals*, *She Stoops to Conquer*, Sheridan's *The Duenna*, and several others, all at Hammersmith; but none of these revivals were quite so successful as *The Way of the World* and *The Beggar's Opera*, though all of them bore the characteristic signature of Nigel Playfair's hand. With Shakespeare, however, he seemed to be unlucky. His *As You Like It*, despite a brilliant Rosalind by Athene Seyler, failed to please, and Bridges-Adams's production of *The Merry Wives of Windsor*, which Playfair also presented one Christmas, at the Lyric, was not greatly successful either, despite the wonderful Mrs Page of Edith Evans. The little Victorian theatre seemed to be especially suited to the eighteenth century, and, notably for *The Beggar's Opera*, it will always be remembered fondly by nostalgic playgoers.

In 1934, at Sadler's Wells, Tyrone Guthrie directed *Love For Love* in the season in which Charles Laughton and Flora Robson starred, and two years later he also directed Wycherley's *The Country Wife* at the Old Vic, though the governors were hard put to it to persuade Lilian Baylis that such a pornographic piece was suitable to enliven the boards of her famous, but strictly moral, theatre. Miss Baylis was a great realist, however, and since the magnificent scenery and costumes (by Oliver Messel) were to be paid for in advance by Gilbert Miller, who proposed to transport the production afterwards to New York, and Edith Evans, always a tremendous favourite at the Old Vic, was to play Lady Fidget, she finally agreed to the revival. Guthrie's direction proved to be as brilliant as the best of Playfair's, and the production carried the Hammersmith tradition to a new phase of liveliness, appealing greatly to the Vic's larger popular audience, who were by this time more ready to enjoy so broad a text after the success of Playfair's previous experiments.

In 1924 (while *The Way of the World* was such a success in London) I had acted at Oxford as Valentine in *Love for Love*, directed by James Bernard Fagan, and Tyrone Guthrie, in the same repertory company, played the part of Jeremy, Valentine's servant. Fagan, who had worked as a younger man with Benson, had been manager of the little Court Theatre in London. There, after the first world war, he had directed a series of classical revivals which were scholarly and delightful, including *Twelfth*

Night, *The Merchant of Venice*, *A Midsummer Night's Dream*, *Othello*, and *Henry IV Part II* (as well as Lennox Robinson's Parnell play *The Lost Leader* and the first production of Shaw's *Heartbreak House*). He had been fortunate, as well as clever, in surrounding himself with a company of players many of whom had learnt their craft with Benson, Poel and Granville-Barker before 1914.

Fagan's London ventures (in 1919–23) were almost the only classic revivals seen in the West End at that time, since most of the larger commercial theatres were then occupied by contemporary plays, thrillers, melodramas and light comedies, many of them of rather indifferent quality; but I fancy that Fagan must have lost money in London, for he gave up the Court and went to Oxford shortly afterwards. Here he presented an admirable series of first-class repertory productions with a young company of quite unknown players. He chose skilfully, for many of his discoveries were destined to become well known to the public shortly afterwards. At Oxford I worked with Flora Robson as well as with Tyrone Guthrie. We only rehearsed each play for a week, however, and the productions were naturally extremely simple and suffered from lack of polish. But *Love for Love* was an immediate success in Oxford, and I remember we had to give several extra performances beyond the advertised number. We gave the play in a very full version, but as our audience consisted largely of dons and the highbrow intelligentsia of North Oxford, the text was easily followed and understood.

When I came to prepare my own revival in 1943, I was amazed to find how much of the dialogue was still familiar. I found that I even remembered the exact words in some of the speeches in my part of Valentine. It seemed necessary, however, to cut the text more drastically than at Oxford, and the problems of setting and style troubled me considerably, for two eighteenth-century

[66]

Angus McBean

KING LEAR
Stratford-on-Avon 1950

Plate 5

KING LEAR
with Fool (David O'Brien)
designed by Isamu Noguchi
Palace Theatre 1955

Norman Parkinson (Condé Nast Publications Ltd)

HAMLET
St James's Theatre, New York
1936

Plate 6

KING
RICHARD II
Queen's Theatre
1938

productions in which I had been concerned shortly before this time – *The School for Scandal* directed for me by Tyrone Guthrie in 1938, and *The Beggar's Opera* (for Glyndebourne) which I myself directed in 1940 – had both, to my mind, suffered from an excess of stylization and lack of unity.

My problem in doing a West End revival of *Love for Love* in 1943 was intensified by the prospect of playing in very large theatres, both in London and in the provinces, and of trying to make the wordy, classic text seem alive and truthful to audiences unfamiliar with this type of dialogue. I was lucky enough to cast the play extremely happily despite war conditions, and I discussed with Leon Quartermaine, who was to play Scandal, how best to set about the direction of it. We both felt that if the actors would all play realistically – and were also stylish enough to wear their clothes and deport themselves with elegance – there was no reason why we might not play the play in a naturalistic style, with the 'fourth wall down' as it were. This was in direct opposition to anything I had ever seen, for, in Playfair's productions, the asides were delivered (as no doubt they were in the eighteenth century) directly to the audience, and there was no attempt at localization in the settings, which were merely drop scenes and wings, and served as a background (but not as a home) for the characters in the play.

Of course I am quite prepared to see a revival of *Love for Love* which is directed in a completely different way from mine, for Congreve himself certainly pictured the play without realistic scenery, and with the asides spoken to the audience, just as Shakespeare always pictured his apron stage and balcony.

Rex Whistler, serving in the Guards and so soon to be tragically killed in the Normandy invasion, met me for only a couple of hours on two occasions, and sketched two settings which were exactly of the kind that I had imagined for the play. Valentine's lodgings, a crowded, panelled room, full of junk, furniture, pictures and statuary; and in contrast, the hall of Foresight's house, with a Thornhill mural and lofty ceiling, arched doorways, and almost empty of furniture. Jeanetta Cochrane, who designed the costumes, insisted on absolute accuracy in the cut of the clothes, and, in Whistler's enforced absence, supervised every detail of the furnishings of the scenes and details of the accessories. Whistler and Miss Cochrane between them were largely responsible for the dignity and beauty of the pictorial side of *Love for Love*, but the style which I finally achieved in the production is, of course, difficult for me to describe or assess. Both Guthrie and I certainly owed a good deal to the influence of Playfair and to that of Fagan too.

I am continually fascinated by the influence of directors and actors upon their immediate successors, and also to observe how fashion and taste change and affect the theatre in the course of a very few years. Painted scenery, for instance, has for some time now been considered old-fashioned, and solidly built architectural sets have taken first place, or, alternatively, skeletal abstract inventions and simplified suggestions of places and background. Even the use of materials for costumes and properties has changed recently, and the texture and style of stage wigs. Make-up has undergone a revolution, partly owing to the innovations of stage lighting (usually dispensing with footlights) as well as through the invention of Max Factor flat pancake, which actors now use for the most part instead of the old sticks of grease-paint. Designers are apt to be more strict in demanding accurate hairstyles, shoes and underclothes than in former days, though they are still defeated by actresses who find these accessories uncomfortable or unbecoming. (No one could succeed in persuading Yvonne Arnaud, in *Love for Love*, to wear corsets, and I remember the indignation of Cecil Beaton, in *Lady Windermere's Fan*, because he could not persuade the ladies to thicken their eyebrows in correct Edwardian fashion.) It is curious how contemporary fashion always seems to affect the wearing of costume and wigs in the theatre. The Edwardian actresses (including Ellen Terry), as one can see from photographs, all contrived to wear the fringes that they thought becoming in private life, whatever character (Beatrice, Portia or Lady Macbeth) they were trying to represent. Modern actresses dislike tight lacing, and fight against wearing any hairstyle of a previous era that they consider does not suit them. Yet the film of *Kermesse Heroïque* (Feyder's production with Françoise Rosay), in which every detail of hair, shoes, ruffs and accessories, meticulously reproduced after the pictures of Franz Hals, was memorably perfect, and should be shown to all young players as a model of how period costume can and should be worn. Today directors who fear they will not be able to teach their actors to wear costume will often by-pass the problem by putting a play into modern dress, and this method, when brilliantly handled, can, of course, be very successful – though personally I cannot believe that an actress looking like the Merry Widow while she impersonates Helen of Troy, or an actor who plays Edmund in *King Lear* dressed (and behaving) like a beatnik, will find it easier to bring these characters convincingly to life.

Nigel Playfair will be chiefly remembered in our theatre for his great influence in popularizing eighteenth-century revivals. I only worked three times under his direction: in *The Insect Play* (Čapek), *Robert E. Lee* (Drinkwater) and, in 1930, in *The Importance of Being Earnest*, between my two Shakespeare seasons at the Old Vic. For this revival Playfair chose a new young designer, Michael Weight, and between them they evolved an extremely simple production in black, white and grey, *à la* Aubrey Beardsley. The scenery was merely a few screens in the same convention, decorative rather than realistic, and there was a minimum of furniture and accessories. I found the final effect too much like a revue for my own taste, and lacking in the opulent stuffiness which the snobbish atmosphere of the Wilde text seems to demand; but like all Playfair's work, the production was clean-cut, fresh and incisive, and I learned to know and love the play and began to conceive many ideas about it that I was able to develop successfully when I came to direct and act in it again nine years later.

When a leading player achieves a consummate style in a classical revival, the whole performance is naturally affected by his or her example. Playfair would no doubt have been the first to acknowledge that his collaboration with Lovat Fraser, and his casting, first of Frederick Ranalow in *The Beggar's Opera*, then of Edith Evans in *The Way of the World*, influenced the way these productions finally developed. Yvonne Arnaud, a brilliant farcical actress (whom I had always remembered for her enchanting Mrs Pepys in Fagan's comedy, *And So To Bed*) brought such skill and experience to the part of Mrs Frail in my *Love for Love*, that the whole cast seemed to discover and develop the right gusto and style from her example. Whistler and Miss Cochrane helped me unfailingly by their knowledge of the manners and customs of the Restoration, and the performance achieved a remarkable unity, after a very hazardous and confused period of rehearsals. It was true that nearly all of us were a good many years too old for the characters we represented but, fortunately, this did not seem to worry anybody who saw the play, though later, in New York, several of the London principals were unable, or unwilling, to go, and the revival had only a mild success there compared to the sensational run in England. But I found I was not able to re-create the spirit of the production successfully a second time. It may be too that the background of the Restoration period was puzzling to an American audience. The behaviour of a corrupt, idle, society, led by a profligate Court, though familiar to every English schoolboy who has read of Charles the Second or the Prince Regent, seems as strange to an audience in the United States as the Molière comedies, so eternally popular in France, which have so seldom succeeded in translation either in England or America.

THE SCHOOL FOR SCANDAL

THE CHARACTERS in classic comedies never seem to do any work. Shakespeare, Congreve, Sheridan and Wilde all wrote amusing studies about people of leisure, and the audiences who came to laugh at these plays were, of course, largely made up of people of leisure too. They enjoyed seeing themselves represented on the stage, whether realistically drawn or presented with satirical exaggeration. From Aristophanes to Molière and, in the last century, from Maugham and Pinero to Chekhov, Coward and Lonsdale, the follies and foibles of moneyed people and their amusing relationships with the servants whom they employed, supplied the writers of comedy with an endless variety of delightful scenes and situations.[1]

Much classic comedy is essentially good-natured. It may also be romantic, sentimental or cynical; often, as in Shakespeare, it is poetic too. Congreve is not brutally malevolent, though he is often both satirical and coarse. Wilde is snobbish but fundamentally good-natured. Sheridan, another Irishman, is neither coarse nor snobbish. He writes with exquisite style and immense

---

[1] I suppose that Barrie's *Admirable Crichton*, in which the servants turn the tables on their masters, was a shrewdly prophetic signpost, when it was written at the beginning of this century, to the coming of the domestic revolution, but I fancy the humour of it would be too snobbish to appeal to an audience today. In time to come it may still perhaps be revived to take its place among the best comedies of the Edwardian era, as indeed it is.

charm, even when he is drawing his most malicious characters.

In *The Way of the World*, Congreve's Lady Wishfort is a kind of fantastic monster, and so are Petulant and Witwoud. Tattle, in *Love for Love*, and the two old men, Sir Sampson Legend and old Foresight, in the same play, seem to be a good deal larger than life, whereas Mrs Candour, Sir Benjamin Backbite, and Crabtree in *The School for Scandal* are absurd, eccentric busybodies, always verging upon caricature without ever quite going over the edge, while the other principal characters are human, natural figures, even though, in the main outline of their behaviour, they live up to the names with which Sheridan has so carefully christened them. It is important to bear this in mind in casting and directing the comedy.

Although his plot is founded on malice, Sheridan's wit is essentially simple and slyly good-natured, and the ending of the play is both moral and sentimental, in the approved taste of the time. Lady Teazle and Charles Surface, the heroine and hero, are charming, reckless, light-hearted characters, both of them victims of their own rashness, and both by the time the play is over have promised to reform.

The action is cleverly devised to exhibit three separate groups of characters in successively contrasting situations, until the four principal persons are finally brought together in the wonderfully constructed fourth act, the famous screen scene. At first the episodes may appear to have been chosen somewhat at random, but they are, in fact, most aptly varied in order to display the characters in amusing situations at different times of day in three completely different households.

Lady Sneerwell, Joseph Surface and the scandal-mongers are first introduced to set the action of the play in motion; then, in the second scene, we are introduced to Sir Peter and Rowley, and immediately afterwards to the first morning quarrel, between Lady Teazle and her husband. The two groups meet at Lady Sneerwell's tea party in the fourth scene. This is not, I think, an evening party, as was the stage tradition for many years. (The scene used often to be an excuse for new elaborate costumes, extra non-speaking characters, and a minuet, for which there is no indication in the text.) Sir Peter leaves the party, and Lady Teazle joins the ladies at cards, after Joseph has been seen making advances both to her and to Maria. Sir Peter, returning home, meets Sir Oliver, Moses is introduced, and the scheme of testing the two Surface brothers is prepared. Later in the evening Lady Teazle also comes home. She has lost two hundred pounds at cards, and has another quarrel with Sir Peter, during which he accuses her of being in love with Charles, on which she makes up her mind to revenge herself by going next day to visit Joseph. The Teazles now leave the stage for a time (the scandal-monger group have been so strongly established that they are given only one more scene, in the last act), and Charles now has two fine showy scenes, with Careless, Moses, Sir Oliver and Rowley to support him. He appears for the first time very late in the play, but he has been mentioned so often in the preceding acts that the audience is impatient for a sight of him, and his good-natured wildness, at home among his cronies, makes a delightful contrast to the sedate manners of the people in the earlier scenes of the play.

Greatly as I admire and respect Sheridan's text, I ventured to make one major change in my own production.[1] This occurs in the fourth act, in which I ventured to adopt a transposition made when the play was directed in London by Sir Herbert Tree some fifty years ago. Whether Tree himself took the hint from an earlier stage tradition I cannot say. The scene between Joseph Surface and Sir Oliver (disguised as Mr Stanley), which Sheridan placed following the screen scene, was played before

[1] See Appendix 3

it in my production. The progress of the action thus seemed to me to move more quickly and to be a less dangerous anticlimax, though admittedly something was lost for Joseph, whose discomfiture *after* the screen scene is more complete (and his odious behaviour to Stanley more rational) in Sheridan's original text. But I tried to make up for this by showing Joseph in a mood of equally irritable impatience because of the delayed arrival of Lady Teazle, and I believe this gave the scene much the same effect as was intended by the author, with an added sense of urgency and expectation.

Ralph Richardson helped me greatly in studying the play and arranging it at our rehearsals. It was his suggestion to divide it into two parts, with only one interval, and to emphasize the different times of day at which the scenes were probably intended to take place, covering a definite period of three days. Unlike Shakespeare, who nearly always indicates clearly in the text where and at what time of day his scenes are meant to occur, Sheridan, with his comparatively new toys – his wings, drop scenes, and candlelight (and directing his own company besides) – did not presumably find it necessary to give many explicit indications of this kind, though the opening scene of *The School for Scandal* is obviously in the morning, the screen scene in the afternoon, and Charles's drinking party at night.

The plots of *The Way of the World* and *Love for Love* are complicated and tedious to follow, largely concerned as they are with seductions, illegitimacy, adultery, the ratifying of wills, and the intrigues over the inherited fortunes of the two young heroines, Millamant and Angelica. In *The School for Scandal* also the young girl, Maria, is a rich heiress, and Joseph Surface (and probably Sir Benjamin Backbite too) plans only to marry her for her money. The prodigal brother Charles wins her, of course, in the end, as a hero should. But one cannot help wondering if his promises of reformation will be carried out, or whether he will not immediately squander his new-found wealth.

Will Sir Peter and his Lady really succeed in living amicably together once the play is done? The mainspring of the comedy is founded on this very question, yet surely the author hardly intends us to be seriously concerned with it once we have left the theatre. And, while we are watching the play, how amusingly he manages the progress of his story, as it moves steadily along from the elegant, but somewhat elaborate, exposition of the earlier scenes to the climax in the fourth act towards which he has been so cunningly directing his principal characters. In this great scene they are all brought together at last. The attempted seduction of Lady Teazle, the wonderfully timed interruptions of Sir Peter and Charles, the farcical poppings in and out, and the final denouement of comedy and pathos, all this is brilliantly conceived. Every facet in the writing and development of the characters is brought to a head by the dramatist with a satin-smoothness of style and craft.

Of course the manners and motives of the play are somewhat strange to us today. Yet how easily we sympathize with the reckless charm of Charles and Lady Teazle and the forthright-ness of jolly old Sir Oliver. How amusingly Sir Peter growls and grumbles, and how we sympathize with his dismay when he discovers his young wife behind the screen. How charmingly naïve is Charles, how smoothly villainous is Joseph, how slyly impertinent the subordinate characters of Snake, Trip and Moses. And while we listen to the gossip of the scandal-mongers about people that we never even see – Tom Saunter, Miss Prim, Mrs Ogle and Colonel Cassino – we smile as we think how little people today have changed in their delight in uncovering the private affairs of their so-called friends and neighbours.

Sheridan has no need for innuendo or coarseness of situation. Here are no bedrooms or china closets conveniently adjacent, as in the plays of Congreve and Wycherley. There is not even a boudoir. Lady Sneerwell's dressing-room is simply used for her levée. Joseph's prim, newly decorated library is in itself a witty background for the attempted seduction of Lady Teazle, and even this episode takes place in an atmosphere of delicate restraint. A finger placed tentatively upon a lady's sleeve is sufficient to convey a wealth of bad intention when accompanied by witty repartee. Only Maria and Charles (and the Teazles in their final reconciliation) are permitted to indulge in formal embraces as the curtain falls. Millamant remarks in Congreve's greatest play, 'Let us be very strange and well-bred'. Sheridan in his masterpiece shows us the very mask of comedy, mocking the shallow pretences that have always sought to cover truth in every age of urban society.[1] It was surely no accident that made him use a screen as the most significant piece of furniture in his play, and inspired him to give the name of Surface to three of his most important characters. In the Oxford Dictionary the phrase, 'There is no trusting appearances' is one of the famous quotations given from the play. Sheridan might well have used it as an alternative title.

[1] In Shakespeare's *Much Ado About Nothing* and *Twelfth Night*, the simple characters reveal the truth and put the artificial ones to shame. Dogberry, Beatrice, and Benedick expose the shallowness of the Prince and Claudio. Sir Toby, Aguecheek, and Fabian expose Malvolio, while Viola shows up the affectations of Olivia and Orsino.

THE IMPORTANCE OF BEING EARNEST

THE COMEDIES of the Restoration period, Sheridan's a century and a half later, and those of Oscar Wilde in the eighteen-nineties, are of course less imaginative and less free, both in conception and execution, than the comedies of Shakespeare, and all of them were intended essentially for a proscenium stage. Their performance demands, both in acting and direction, a considerable understanding of the period in which they were written, and some degree of urban sophistication from the audience. They are city plays, and, though there are country scenes in some of them, those scenes represent the country seen very much through city eyes.

Shakespeare lived, probably, as much in the country as he did in London. Many of his comedies are pastoral in scene and atmosphere, but in his day the cities were so small compared to ours that the juxtaposition in his plays of scenes of town and country life, court and woodland, inn yard, castle and seashore, give to their action a wonderful freedom of movement and variety of exposition.

After the Restoration and the introduction of the picture stage, plays came to be written which could be sustained throughout in a single mood. Three or four long acts took the place of short scenes. Audiences began to enjoy seeing people on the stage behaving exactly as they themselves behaved at home, only saying more amusing things, against a background of imitative scenery and realistic accessories.

[78]

But playwrights of genius cannot be bounded by convention. The mad scene of Valentine in Congreve's *Love for Love*, Worthing's interview with Lady Bracknell in *The Importance of Being Earnest*, and his arrival in mock mourning in the second act of the latter play – these scenes have a kind of poetic fantasy, though, of course, they are comic scenes as well. The invention of the author seems to blossom into a kind of inspired lunacy which is so exquisitely original as to carry the plays in which they occur to a brilliant peak of nonsense. They are incomparable examples of their kind, scenes of classic farce. The screen scene in *The School for Scandal*, on the other hand, though equally brilliant in construction, is essentially realistic.

We shall never know whether Wilde wrote his last play meaning it to be a stage reproduction of high life as he knew it at the time in London. It may be that the touches which make the play most memorable only occurred to him as afterthoughts. We know him to have been the most wonderful extempore talker, but it is possible too that before he went to a party he did a little homework first (just as an actor sometimes does) and was ready with some of the good things he proposed to say, even if he was not sure of the order in which he was going to say them. No doubt, too, he was stimulated by his own wit, and one good remark suggested another, till the best one, the cherry on top of the cake, came to him suddenly in a flash of inspiration. But he was an admirable and thorough craftsman too. The construction of this, his best play, is careful and precise, though the author does not hesitate to make use of a set of stock characters and several well-worn devices of farce to carry his plot to a satisfactory conclusion, just as Shakespeare, Sheridan, and Congreve were not above using borrowed plots, slapstick, and conventional misunderstandings to keep the action spinning along to the usual pairing-off of couples at the end of their comedies.

The Importance of Being Earnest begins in an apparently realistic atmosphere. The characters behave and talk in the languid, pointed, self-conscious manner of their day. They are witty, cultured, idle and wealthy. Even Lane, Algernon's manservant, has caught some of his master's wit, adding a pinch of his own, and replies to questions with epigrams uttered in tones of perfect deferential gravity. Everybody is solemn, correct, polite. The bachelors only loll or smoke or cross their legs when they are alone. Whenever ladies are present, they sit with straight backs and conduct themselves with irreproachable exactitude, hitching their trousers before they sit down, stripping off their gloves, shooting their cuffs. Their hats are worn at exactly the right angle, their canes carried with an air of studied negligence. They have never been seen in Bond Street or Piccadilly without top-hats and frock-coats.

Algy, in the country, is dressed to kill. But he must not kill the comedy by a costume verging upon caricature. A correct country suit of the period will be quite amusing enough to our modern eyes. Miss Prism and Doctor Chasuble are stock figures of farce, the spinster governess and the country rector, but they must be simple and sincere in their playing, not exaggeratedly ridiculous. If they are well acted, they can have great charm – Prism, in her final scene of discomfiture, may even achieve a touch of pathos. The comedy, verging upon fantasy, occasionally spills over into farce, but it must never degenerate into knockabout. In act two it is traditional for Worthing to produce from his breast-pocket a black-edged handkerchief. (We do not know if this was the invention of Wilde, or of George Alexander, who created the part. I suspect the latter, for there is no mention of it in the printed text.) The actor must not handle this continually, or he will certainly distract from the dialogue and gain cheap laughter from the audience. Used once or twice, the invention is legitimate. Flourished once too often, it may destroy the elegance of the author's exquisite invention. The scene with the muffins, at the end of the same act, should be played deliberately and with great seriousness. Here again, the actors must not indulge themselves too much. If they snatch and shout and talk with their mouths full, the decorum, the deadly importance of the triviality is lost. They are greedy, determined, but still exasperatedly polite.

Cecily is first cousin to Alice in Wonderland – the same backboard demureness, the same didactic manner, the echoes of remarks she has copied from her elders and her governess. Gwendolen is perhaps more difficult for an actress to hit off correctly, but we may find her prototype in the cartoons of George du Maurier in *Punch*. But her affectations must be of Society; she should not have the 'Greenery Yallery Grosvenor Gallery' airs which Gilbert satirized in *Patience*. She is bored and elegant, with an occasional flash of individuality peeping out from under the overwhelming layers of her mother's condescension and snobbishness, which she frequently echoes in her own remarks.

Lady Bracknell is not called Augusta for nothing. She is never put out or surprised and she is never angry. But she is frequently disapproving, and almost always annihilating. If the author were anyone but Wilde, she would be unanswerable. She moves slowly and seldom. She is beautifully dressed and carries herself superbly. Her every accessory – veil, gloves, parasol, châtelaine, bag and shoes – should be worn with a perfection of detail that has become second nature to her. It is impossible to conceive her (or her daughter either) except *en grande tenue*.

The pace of the comedy must be leisurely and mannered; and everybody must, of course, speak beautifully, but the wit must somehow have an air of spontaneity, and the text must be studied and spoken so as to arouse a cumulative effect of laughter from the audience. That is to say, it may be sometimes necessary to sacrifice laughs on certain witty lines in order that a big laugh may come at the end of a passage, rather than to extract two or three small ones in between, which may dissipate the sense and hold up the progress of the dialogue. There are, if anything, too many funny lines, and the actor may easily ruin a passage by allowing the audience to laugh too soon. The following celebrated sally in the first act, for instance:

> JACK: My dear Algy, you talk exactly as if you were a dentist. It is very vulgar to talk like a dentist when one isn't a dentist. It produces a false impression.
> ALGERNON: Well, that is exactly what dentists always do.

If the actor playing Jack allows the audience to laugh after the words, 'It produces a false impression', Algernon's reply will fall flat and seem redundant. Actors with expert pace and timing will hurry the dialogue, Algernon breaking in quickly with his line, so that the audience will not laugh until he has spoken it.

A certain amount of 'business' is surely justifiable. In my own productions of the play I have introduced a persistently warbling bird in the garden scene, rudely interrupting Gwendolen in the midst of one of her most pregnant observations, a church clock to herald Worthing's entrance in mourning and to chime four o'clock as tea is punctually served and, in the third act, a step-ladder to the high bookcase in which Ernest seeks for the Army Lists, thus providing him with a dominating if precarious position for the moment of final denouement. But such interpolations must be discreetly introduced, and not allowed to disturb the brilliant flow of dialogue or drown an important line with irrelevant laughter.

The play can be mounted either in the correct period, 1895, or, at the producer's discretion, in a slightly later year – but not I think later than 1906. Motley, the designers who worked

JOSEPH SURFACE
in *The School for Scandal*
Theatre Royal, Haymarket
1962

Plate 7

N WORTHING
he Importance
eing Earnest
be Theatre 1939

GAEV   *John Timber*
with Varya (Dorothy Tutin) and Anya (Judi Dench)
in *The Cherry Orchard*, Aldwych Theatre 1961

Plate 8   THOMAS MENDIP
with Jennet Jourdemayne (Pamela Brown) and Richard (Richard Burton)
in *The Lady's Not for Burning*, Globe Theatre 1940   *Angus McBean*

for me, decided that Lady Bracknell would look more imposing in the great hats of the early Edwardian era than in the small bonnets worn by the older generation in the nineties, and this was the main reason we finally chose the later period for our production. Also the furnishings of the rooms at the later date, heavier and more ornate, seemed to us to provide a more amusingly lavish and crowded background. But Algy's room might well be decorated with blue and white china, Japanese fans, Aubrey Beardsley drawings and spindly bamboo furniture, with the morning-room of the last act a comfortable contrast of mid-Victorian solidity. Certainly the garden must be pretty and profuse with roses, the tea-table groaning with lace, silver and masses of food, and Worthing must be the only character allowed to use the centre entrance, appearing with stately processional gloom upon the sunlit scene.

It is not easy to achieve the style, the lightness, the apparent ease which the play demands. Above all it is difficult to act it with a deadly seriousness, yet to keep an inner consciousness of fun, the fun with which one plays seriously a very elaborate practical joke.

The comedy must originally have been thought funny because it tilted so brilliantly at contemporary society. The people who laughed at it were, many of them, laughing at themselves, reproduced with only very slight exaggeration upon the stage. Today we laugh at the very idea that such types could ever have existed; at the whole system – the leaving of cards, chaperons, official proposals of marriage, the ceremony of meals, the ridiculously exaggerated values of birth, rank and fashion.

But there is a danger that the actors of today, lacking real types to draw from, will turn the comedy into wild caricature, and the audience, even if they do not know the reason, will then find the piece contrived, silly and overdrawn. The performance needs to be correct though not dry, leisurely but not dragged, solemn yet full of sparkle. Above all it is an agreeable play. The brittle crackling staccato of Noël Coward, the smart rudeness of Frederick Lonsdale, this was not wit as Wilde conceived it. In his plays nobody is nervous, impatient, catty, or ill-natured. The 'lower classes' are spoken of patronizingly but not contemptuously. Even Lady Bracknell's stern summons of Prism in the final scene is firm without being cruel. The girls conduct their elegant quarrel with the highest good breeding. No one must ever lose their tempers or their poise. The movement throughout must be smooth, stylish (but not balletic, as so often occurs when actors and directors try to create a period sense) and the more elegantly the actors give and take the more will the intrinsic quality of the wit emerge, as the grave puppet characters utter their delicate cadences and spin their web of preposterously elegant sophistication.

CHEKHOV PLAYS

CONSTANTIN – TUSENBACH – TRIGORIN –
VERSHININ – GAEV

M Y SLAV ANCESTRY, on my father's side, may account
for my love of the plays of Chekhov,[1] and I have been
closely involved in seven different revivals of three of his most
famous plays, acting, on different occasions, two different parts
in each of them.

When *The Cherry Orchard* was produced at Oxford in 1924,
the general public was only just beginning to appreciate the
play for the first time. When Fagan brought it to London
(sponsored by Nigel Playfair) the press was extremely mixed.
Only James Agate championed it in his dramatic column in the
Sunday Times and recommended it over the radio. Trofimov
was the first part in which I felt somewhat released from my
youthful self-consciousness. It began to dawn on me that a
performance must somehow be projected from within oneself as
well as by the more obvious efforts of external impersonation. I
became aware of the need for flexibility of mood and accurate
orchestration of dialogue in a complicated ensemble, the value
of pauses, and the art of listening.

Fagan's production of *The Cherry Orchard* was somewhat
clumsy and tentative, for we were a young and inexperienced
company, though sincere, and there had been only time at

[1] See Appendix 4

Oxford for very short rehearsals. *The Seagull*, when I came to play in it shortly afterwards, seemed to me a more conventional kind of play, and I felt I understood it a little better, at least as regards the melodramatic side of the plot (the jealousies, quarrelling, and Constantin's suicide at the end), though my own performance was somewhat highly strung, and I wore my black Russian blouse and boots with what I imagined to be a becoming air of romantic gloom. Valerie Taylor's Nina was a beautiful performance and I took a little credit for her success in the part. I well remember taking her back to my parents' house (where I was still living at the time) one evening after finishing rehearsal in the theatre, to work with her on the great scene in the last act. We both knew that the director had given us little help in this vital passage, and I felt certain that my ideas about it were valid if I could persuade her to work on them with me. For the first time I was convinced that I might one day aspire to become a director myself.

Komisarjevsky saw *The Seagull*, and ridiculed the production, though he evidently liked my performance sufficiently to engage me for his forthcoming season at the Barnes Theatre – a small house, across Hammersmith Bridge, with an ill-equipped, tiny stage, and a small auditorium without balconies. Here Komisarjevsky directed six or seven distinguished plays in succession over a period of only a few months. He was responsible for everything: direction, casting, lighting, scenery and dresses. In spite of a very perverse sense of humour and an unpredictable temperament, his resourcefulness, artistry and authority over his actors held me completely fascinated. He was a born teacher, a sensitive musician, and a fine designer. Under his influence, the young Charles Laughton, Peggy Ashcroft, Jean Forbes-Robertson and I, four of his most ardent pupils and admirers, began to find success, encouraged by his shrewd advice and criticism.

[86]

In *The Three Sisters*, the first play I was in at Barnes, I played the young Baron Tusenbach. Of course I was then a novice, and it is difficult to judge, after so many years, how the Komisarjevsky *Three Sisters* compared with that directed by Michel Saint-Denis in 1938, and with the performance given by the Moscow Arts Theatre on their visit to London only a few years ago. The Barnes production was certainly more romantic than the other two; the play was dressed in 1880 costumes, and Tusenbach, shorn of the lines about his ugliness, was played (by Komisarjevsky's express directions) as a romantic juvenile. Perhaps he thought it was the only way that I would be able to act it successfully. When I questioned him about the 'ugly' lines being cut, he shrugged his expressive shoulders and said, 'My dear boy, the English public always demand a love interest.' But I remember feeling somewhat suspicious even then. Years later, the young Michael Redgrave, who played the same part in the Saint-Denis production, made an outstanding success of his performance, wearing gold-rimmed spectacles and a ridiculous straw hat. He was infinitely moving, and amusing too, especially in his drunk scene, and in his stammering farewell to Irina before going to the duel in the last act, I realized that the Russian director had led me deliberately in a wrong direction.

There were many beautiful things in his production all the same. The lighting of the third act (the scene in the girl's bedroom with the fire-engines passing outside) was strikingly effective. The scene ended with the shadow of Olga thrown on to the screen behind the bed as she tried to comfort the weeping Irina. The whole setting for the play, a permanent arrangement of flats, brilliantly rearranged for each of the four acts, evoked a simple yet convincing atmosphere of different times of year, and also managed to convey, on the very shallow stage, a remarkable effect of depth, and of different rooms opening one out of another into a garden. I remember our first rehearsals in someone's Bloomsbury flat, with the floor marked out in bewildering lines of coloured chalk – the groupings, entrances and exits all most accurately planned – though at first we could none of us imagine why we were being shuffled about in such intricate patterns of movement.

Komisarjevsky talked little, and allowed us all to flounder about for several rehearsals trying to discover character for ourselves. His few remarks tended to be ironic, subtle and suggestive, and he was masterly in his use of pauses, so necessary and so effective in Chekhov. But he could be very cold to players whom he did not like, sometimes ignoring them almost completely, and even cutting their lines or putting them at a disadvantage in bad positions. In fact, he had all the intolerant waywardness of his undeniable virtuosity. After his success at Barnes he complained that managers only asked him to direct Russian plays, but (with the exception of *Musical Chairs*, Ronald Mackenzie's Chekhovian tragi-comedy, which he directed for me in 1931 with brilliant success) I think he never did better work, in England at any rate, than during those Barnes seasons in the twenties.

Besides the Chekhov revivals there, he also directed Andreyev's *Katerina* (in which I played a middle-aged man for the first time) and several other Russian plays, notably Gogol's *The Government Inspector* and later *Paul the First* (at the Court Theatre), with George Hayes and Charles Laughton, but I did not appear in either of these productions.

In 1936, when I asked him to direct *The Seagull* for me, I was under contract to Bronson Albery, and this was the first Chekhov production in the West End to be given the full honours of a star cast and expensive décor. Komisarjevsky behaved with his usual mixture of charm and devilry. He designed an unnecessarily expensive set for the first act (leaves for the trees made of real silk), scoffed at the 'commercial management', and gave a long talk to us before the first reading decrying the methods of the British theatre in general and West End actors in particular. Edith Evans showed some resentment at this attitude, but he soon won her over with a dazzling display of charm, and from the moment when, at an early rehearsal, she paused to listen to the music across the lake in the first act (and paused longer than any other actress would dare to do) she won his uncompromising allegiance. As Arcádina she gave one of her most inspired performances. Komisarjevsky insisted that I played Trigorin as a smartly dressed, blasé gigolo, and many people criticized me for this reading of the part, quoting Stanislavsky's famous remark that Trigorin ought to wear an old hat and shabby check trousers. Komisarjevsky may have rejected such a Bohemian get-up for this very reason, since he detested conventional tradition. I was somewhat suspicious at the time that he had revised his views on the character to fit my recently acquired status as a West End star, and his idea that the London public would certainly expect me to be glamorous at all costs, but, just as with *The Three Sisters*, his direction of the play as a whole was brilliant, and he achieved a critical as well as a popular success.

I saw his productions of *Ivanov* and *Uncle Vanya* at Barnes. Both of these were memorable, but I missed his *Cherry Orchard* (with Charles Laughton as Epihodov, and Martita Hunt as Charlotta). It would have been fascinating to compare it with the other three productions (Fagan's, that of Saint-Denis and my own) with which I have been associated before and since.

The last time I worked with him was in New York in 1948, when he directed *Crime and Punishment*, an adaptation by Rodney Ackland in which I was to play Raskolnikov, as I had done the season before in London under Anthony Quayle's direction. Komisarjevsky did not really believe in the version (he

would have preferred to make his own) nor did he like the
setting, which we had brought over from the London production
(again he would have preferred to design a completely different
one himself). He also took a dislike to a number of players in
the big cast. The production was a failure, and his work in it
half-hearted, largely, I think, for the reasons I have already
stated, though nothing could shake me in my personal affection
for him or in my admiration for his diversity of talents. His
work in *Musical Chairs* was masterly, and he handled me as
brilliantly in it as he did the young author. On the other hand
his production of *The Maitlands* – Mackenzie's last play, produced after his death in 1934 – was a great disappointment.

Michel Saint-Denis had directed me as Noah in Obey's play in
1934 when I was still contracted to Bronson Albery. In 1938,
when I went into management myself, I invited him to direct
The Three Sisters in my season at the Queen's Theatre. The repertory company I had engaged already included Peggy Ashcroft,
Michael Redgrave, Glen Byam Shaw, Harry Andrews, Alec
Guinness, George Devine, Leon Quartermaine, Frederick
Lloyd, Angela Baddeley and myself – and I invited Gwen
Ffrangcon-Davies to play Olga and Carol Goodner to play
Masha – so the cast was a very distinguished one. Also we had
eight weeks for our rehearsals, instead of the usual three or four,
and this was an enormous advantage as it turned out, though at
first the prospect of such a long time of preparation somewhat
alarmed us all. Saint-Denis brought very full notes to rehearsal.
Every move and piece of business was prepared beforehand on
paper, and the play was placed very quickly in consequence.
This is a method I have never been able to achieve myself,
though I have greatly admired it in masters like Komisarjevsky,
Barker and Saint-Denis. Tyrone Guthrie and Peter Brook, on
the other hand, are inclined to improvise more spontaneously,
as I do myself, and seem to allow the actors a greater share of

liberty in finding their own development and inventing their characterizations on their own lines. Talented players are usually able to work in many different ways, and I do not believe that any set of rules can be laid down. I had not thought to work again in Chekhov so rewardingly as in my early days with Komisarjevsky. However, in the Saint-Denis *Three Sisters* everything seemed to contribute to bring about an achievement of which we were all extremely proud. Many people remember that production as being of the most perfect examples of team-work ever presented in London, and even the performance of the Moscow Arts Theatre in the same play twenty years later was, in my opinion (and that of many others too) no better than ours, despite the wonderful acting of Gribov as the Doctor and the brilliant quality of the company as a whole.

I know I was not very satisfied at the time with my own acting as Vershinin, and there was some discussion beforehand as to whether I might not be better cast as the brother Andrey. But during the course of the run I gradually became more at ease in the part of the Colonel, and thought I had improved my performance considerably. I only remember now the pleasure I derived in presenting the play under my own management, and the discomfort we men suffered in our tight military uniforms, with huge greatcoats, in very hot weather. Of the long rehearsals I can remember little, save that we never found them tedious and became daily more involved in the subtleties which they enabled us to develop in such harmony. Before the run was over we invited our colleagues in the profession to a special midnight performance of the play, and their response on that occasion was unforgettable.

After these rewarding experiences with foreign directors, I was naturally eager to experiment in trying my own hand at directing a Chekhov play, but it was not until 1954 that I was asked to stage *The Cherry Orchard*. In the other Chekhov productions it had always been found necessary to re-phrase many of the speeches in the Garnett translations, though Komisarjevsky had himself made his own translation of *The Seagull* for his 1936 production. In 1954 I worked with a Russian friend, and managed to make a new version of *The Cherry Orchard*, which seemed to me to be more colloquial than any of the older published translations and easier for the actors to speak.[1] From this production too, I have very happy memories of fine performances, especially the Varya (Pauline Jameson), Trevor Howard's Lopahin, and the beautiful acting of Gwen Ffrangcon-Davies as Madame Ranevsky and of Esmé Percy as her brother Gaev.

Playing Gaev myself in 1961, under Saint-Denis's direction, I found it difficult to forget the perfection of Esmé Percy's acting and that of Leon Quartermaine, another fine Gaev. But the character is delightfully rewarding to the actor, and suited me, I think, better than any other in which Saint-Denis has directed me; at least I enjoyed working for him more on this occasion than ever before.

English actors certainly seem to have a special gift for playing Chekhov. Perhaps we are more nearly in sympathy with the Russian temperament than we imagine. The plays are unique in the sense of reality which they create when one is acting in them. One seems to become part of the life of a group of people as well as an individual stage character. Each of the four acts has its own particular mood and progression, like the movements of a symphony. The sounds and pauses give endless opportunities for subtle orchestration, the long speeches are sometimes eloquent, sometimes declamatory, the short ones capable of producing a delicious effect of comic inconsequentiality or touching simplicity. Though the author is writing so intimately

[1] Published by Heinemann 1963 and Theatre Arts Books, New York, 1963.

of an age and manner of living that is gone for ever, the impartial, delicate perceptiveness of his genius has created such human relationships and such vivid, universal types, that one finds oneself relaxing, in portraying his characters, in a way that is quite unlike one's feelings in acting the plays of any other dramatist.

Playing Chekhov in the twenties and thirties was to us like discovering a new form, just as the young actors of today have been discovering a new form in the 'theatre of the absurd' dramatists. It is difficult to appreciate the subtleties of a new form of writing unless one takes the trouble to study it and give it a chance to make its gradual effect upon one's own preconceived notions of what a play should be. This applies equally, of course, to modern music, sculpture, poetry, films and architecture. One tries to remember the first time one heard a Beethoven symphony, saw a Shakespeare play, tasted oysters or caviare, beer or whisky, or looked at a picture by one of the Post-Impressionists or a piece of sculpture by Henry Moore.

It is grossly unfair, of course, to dismiss an author because he is difficult to understand at first, just as it is equally dangerous to be impressed or become falsely enthusiastic with regard to new work unless one can feel a sincere conviction that one can bring oneself to tackle it with real enthusiasm. It was with this kind of enthusiasm that we first came to love the Chekhov plays at Oxford and Barnes in 1924. The beauty of the Olivier *Uncle Vanya* at Chichester, so successful in two seasons, is yet another example of Chekhov's appeal to English audiences, and of the response evoked by his genius from the finest of our English actors and directors.

A PHOBIA OF FESTIVALS

ELSINORE (Hamlet) – BULAWAYO (Richard II) –
BOSTON (Benedick)

Denmark. Spring 1939.

I HAVE BEEN INVITED by the Danish Government to
play Hamlet at the Castle at Elsinore, and fly over to Copen-
hagen to discuss it and see the courtyard where we are to play. I
have never been in an aeroplane before, and have no idea of the
many thousands of miles I am to travel by air in the years to
come.

The stone castle is disappointing, and Hamlet's grave is said
to be a fake. It is even supposed to contain a cat. But everybody
is very agreeable. A charming old lady, sitting next to me at
luncheon smoking a small cigar, remarks off-handedly, 'If war
should break out the Germans would walk into our country in
no time. We have no defences.'

July

We play *Hamlet* for a week at the Lyceum Theatre, London,
Irving's old home, after which it is to be turned into a dance hall.
Our setting – designed for Elsinore to be used out of doors –
does not look very well in a closed theatre, but playing there is
a moving experience, although I am as usual exhausted by long
rehearsals and various technical complications. My fine

company of actors, many of them dear friends with whom I have worked many times before, leaves for Denmark ahead of me by ship, and, when I arrive next day by air, they are gathered, discreetly giggling, to greet me on the steps as I am driven up to the hotel, where, to my great embarrassment, a small cannon is fired in my honour. The weather is extremely wet, and our scenery, set up in the Courtyard of the Castle of Kronborg, looks rather like a sad Punch and Judy show. The banners which flank it are huge and made of painted canvas. They flap noisily in the wind, despite being fairly firmly lashed to the stage. After a night of steady rain they look still more dingy and woebegone. The supers do not understand English, and after some hours of fruitless struggle with an inadequate interpreter I decide to reduce their number as much as possible. We dress in small stone rooms round the courtyard, but smoking is strictly forbidden. Two soldiers with heavy boots and with fire-extinguishers strapped on their backs tramp up and down on the heavy flagstones during the performance and burst into our dressing-rooms at intervals to make sure that no one is disobeying this stupid rule.

It is cold and rains almost every day. The audiences are enthusiastic but sporadic. I hate being able to see them so clearly, as the play begins in daylight. We feel defenceless, with our painted faces, until half-way through the evening when the artificial lights are turned on. The ghost scenes, coming at the beginning of the play, seem to us utterly lacking in atmosphere, and the fact that this must also have been the case in Shakespeare's Globe gives us little consolation. Umbrellas begin to go up during the 'rogue and peasant slave' soliloquy. Somebody rushes towards me down the aisle – am I to be assassinated? No, somebody's umbrella is obscuring the stage from the lady in the row behind, and she indignantly demands that it be lowered immediately.

Two performances are cancelled because of the bad weather. One evening it is still and warm at last, so Ophelia dresses her wig carefully with hair lotion, and behold, a halo of gnats buzzes round her head, as she enters for the Nunnery Scene, and I have great difficulty in keeping a straight face. At another and chillier performance Polonius hisses to me as he leaves the stage, 'The Queen is so cold!' and I enter to my Mother to find her seated regally in her chair with a plaid rug laid across her knees.

The people in the hotel get rather cross with us, and no wonder, for a wild epidemic of practical joking has broken out. The cannon from the front garden has been smuggled upstairs, and is suddenly found to be blocking a corridor. A hen is squawking in someone's bedroom. When I retire for the night I find four people waiting for me tucked up in my bed (including Ophelia), and, when I get up next morning, I open the door to my sitting-room, and a drawer, carefully balanced on top of it, falls on to my head. Two admiring ladies from England, conspicuous in brightly coloured head-scarves, keep moving their seats so as to sit right in front of me in all my principal scenes. This makes me very self-conscious, and I change my moves to thwart them, playing Box and Cox, while Rosencrantz and Guildenstern, moving tentatively to different positions from the ones that have been rehearsed, have to guess where they will find me by the next cue. Midnight bathing in the icy sea is forced on me by the heartier members of the company, and I see the stage-manager, stripped to his underclothes, toddling wildly down the jetty so as to escape being thrown into the water from the beach. One morning we are invited to unveil a plaque to Shakespeare and put on our best clothes to perform the ceremony. We are herded beforehand into a small schoolroom with children's desks, where we have to listen to a twenty-minute speech. We hear our own names recurring at intervals amid a rigmarole of incomprehensible Danish. The orator is a Ustinov-like professor with a long white beard. He keeps slipping off the tiny rostrum, almost disappearing beneath the desk, only to pop up again a minute later with a new flow of rhetoric, while we shake with irrepressible hysteria.

The smørresbrød, which seemed so delicious the first day, begins to become repellent to our voracious appetites. Someone brings me a notice which has been translated, and I rashly read it aloud to the company at supper without first reading it to myself. The critic has made a most insulting remark about my leading lady, but it is too late. We are all horrified and embarrassed, but she roars with laughter, for which I cannot sufficiently admire her.

We earn some critical praise for our performance, but I do not find myself deriving much pleasure from the experience. It marks for me the end of ten years of good luck in the theatre, from the time when I first played leading parts in Shakespeare at the Old Vic, through my seasons at the New Theatre under Bronson Albery, up to my first success in New York as Hamlet in 1936, and my subsequent season of management at the Queen's Theatre two years later. So many of us in the Elsinore *Hamlet* company have been together many times during those exciting years, and I think we all feel some kind of premonition of violent change. We are all grown up now and ready to go our separate ways. It is like the last day at school, but we do not altogether look forward to the holidays. A strange sort of sadness alternates with the grumbling and practical joking during the weeks we are in Denmark, and there is a curious end-of-term melancholy as we pack up and say good-bye. It is only eight weeks later that war will be declared.

Bulawayo 1953

I am invited to the Rhodes Centenary Festival and, having just directed a production of *Richard II*, with Paul Scofield as the King, at the Lyric Theatre, Hammersmith, in London, I decide to take the play to Southern Rhodesia with most of the same company, playing the title role myself.

The others go ahead in a small plane, and have a long and highly enjoyable flight lasting several days. I rashly choose to leave later by Comet with my manager. We land at Rome, in almost unbearably hot weather, breaking a wheel in the undercarriage with a tremendous bump. The airport is in chaos as the Queen Mother is expected hourly on her return from opening the Rhodes Festival (where she has nearly been frozen to death, we hear, in her summer frocks), and everything has been cleared in preparation for her, so we are all herded into buses, and sent off to spend an unpleasant twelve hours in a hotel. We are told not to go to bed in case our relief plane should arrive during the night. We spend a sulphurous twenty-four hours in Rome and proceed on our journey late the next evening. The Comet shoots upwards with terrifying noises, though it is completely steady once we are in the air. But we are given no opportunity to settle down and sleep in the plane, as we come down every two hours to refuel and feed. We suffer great discomfort from indigestible meals and lack of sleep. In Khartoum we are blinded by a sandstorm, but there is a beautiful green and gold sunrise at Entebbe. We arrive at Livingstone at last in the middle of the morning, nearly two days late, and I go to bed for three hours exhausted, but hasten to get up again in order to see the Victoria Falls, which are enormously impressive. After a short night's sleep we are awakened by a sinister African wrapped in a blanket and holding a lantern, who rouses us at 5.45 a.m. in order that we may reach Bulawayo in a small aircraft by 8.30. There we are met by officials who obviously resent the untimeliness of our arrival almost as much as we do. It is terribly cold, and our summer clothes are quite inadequate. The hotel is imposing, new, but chaotically inefficient. It is full of tourists, and nearly all the trained waiters have been seduced away from it by higher wages to work instead at the Festival Night Club. We ring for coffee, and an hour later tea arrives. No spoons, as apparently they are always being stolen by the servants. We are wakened, despite our indignant protests, at 6.30 every morning with large cups of strong tea. The Exhibition, when we go to look at it, is quite attractively laid out, on a huge plain. Icy winds sweep over it continually. The theatre is unheated and seats 3,000 people on a raked stone floor with no balconies. The proscenium is as wide as the Festival Hall in London, and our poor little sets from Hammersmith look like children's screens, so we mask them as best we can with enormous curtains. But it still takes us five minutes, or so it seems, to cross the stage, and all the entrances and exits have to be rearranged in the shortest possible time. Our costumes are fortunately warm and thick, but the audience, scattered but undaunted, sit with rugs over their knees, and we can almost hear their teeth chattering. There is nowhere at all to eat after the performance except at the night club (with dancing and a floor show), which is ruinously expensive. The hotel proffers nothing but some stale sandwiches, and we find ourselves, late at night, shivering in our light overcoats while we consume hot dogs from a naphtha-lit stall in the chilly, wind-blown street.

Among happier memories is a visit to the grave of Rhodes in the Matoppo Hills – memorably simple and impressive – and the pleasure of meeting a little company of African actors in my dressing-room after one of the performances. They had never seen a play acted by white people before, and their

H

delight and graceful appreciation was extremely touching. For the first time, I believe, on this occasion, a few seats were made available to Africans, though I was told that this fact must not be used for publication. Later I visited Durban and two of the big game reserves for a fortnight's holiday, which almost made up for the rigours and disappointments of the Festival.

Boston Festival 1959

I had always hoped to take my Stratford production of *Much Ado About Nothing* to the United States. Now I was asked to open it in Boston, in August, at a newly built Festival Theatre, for two weeks, and then to come in for a limited season to New York.

Boston has always been one of my favourite cities in America, but I had not realized that the heat there can be as tropical (and almost as demoralizing) as in Washington and New York, where I have sweated miserably during other summer visits.

I am taken to see the theatre, which is beside the Charles River, twelve miles outside Boston and fairly close to Harvard. To my dismay, it consists of a circus tent with canvas walls, a (fairly) solid roof and an extremely wide but shallow stage. The surrounding meadows are still in the process of being ploughed up by bulldozers; the auditorium is semi-circular with raked canvas chairs, and behind the scenes there is a narrow open passage, with some fifteen dressing-rooms opening on it with wooden partitions in between them, and two lavatories, for a company of forty. The expression of alarm on my face as the photographers snap me taking in these details faithfully records my dismay and disappointment.

In the evening I go to see a performance of *Macbeth*, which now occupies the tent until our production is ready. The players are pretty well defeated by the conditions – indifferent acoustics, bad loudspeakers, and microphones distorting speech, sound effects and incidental music. Some of the direction is interesting, but an attempt to bring the play forward by means of entrances and exits through the aisles among the audience, only serves to make confusion worse confounded.

We rehearse for three weeks in an old theatre in the city, mercifully air-conditioned, as the temperature is in the nineties and seems likely to remain so. The clammy heat, strongly reminiscent of Bombay and Singapore (where I played Hamlet in 1945), exhausts me considerably. Still, the company works with a will, and I begin to be quite pleased with the result.

We arrive in the tent at last. Our beautiful Stratford scenery has been badly copied in America, and looks disappointingly like an Italian cafeteria; the lighting is very indifferent, and at matinées the sunshine comes in through the chinks of the roofed canvas so strongly that we might as well be playing in the open air. Our music (taped of course) sounds hideously strident, and every aeroplane, boat and car which passes, above or on one side or the other, interrupts the performance with such insistence and so many varieties of noises that we can barely remember our lines.

A bulldozer breaks a water pipe which is laid on for our water supply, and we can neither drink nor wash (on a matinée day too, when we are in the place for a full eight hours). After a great deal of confusion, the local fire brigade arrives to pump in a supply out of the river.

I am asked to sign autographs between the performances for a visiting party of blind people, and demur, as there will be little time to rest. The curtain then rises on the matinée to a half-empty house. Ten minutes later the blind people arrive and are escorted to their seats. This done, the usherettes sink wearily into the empty chairs in the front row and yawn at us and buff their nails. People whose seats are in the direct rays of the sun, shining remorselessly through the gaps in the canvas sides, move about, changing their chairs to get into the shade. The actors keep escaping out of their dressing-rooms to gasp for air on the river bank, some half-naked, some half in costume. The girls' elaborate dresses are soiled as they drag their trains in the long grass, and people cannot be found and miss their entrances. One of the actresses slips in front and outrages me by trying to photograph the play from the front in a scene in which she does not appear herself. She is severely reprimanded and retires sulkily to her dressing-room which, in spite of having to share it with two others, she has further encumbered with her two small children whom she has brought along for the afternoon.

A cloudburst descends during the last act, and the open passage is deep in water. We pick our way from dressing-rooms to stage and battle on with the final scene, not a word of which can be heard, as the rain is crashing down on the solid top of the roof where it drums and reverberates unceasingly and drips through the gaps in the canvas. The aisles are running with water, and the audience sit, with their feet tucked under them, preparing to plunge out at the earliest opportunity, with umbrellas at the ready.

Boston after the play is dead and sinister. The grand hotel where we are staying offers lobster sandwiches and scotch, a diet which becomes somewhat monotonous and indigestible, especially eaten in one's bedroom at midnight like a dormitory feast. The streets are full of bums and down-and-outs, and the all-night cafés across the Common are dirty and full of louche characters of all kinds. I am hardly surprised that the project of a real theatre, supposed to be built on the site of the tent during the following year, does not seem to have materialized since our visit. Why an outdoor place should have been chosen when Boston has three or four excellent theatres, two at least with air-conditioning, and all closed for the summer months, passes my comprehension.

Is it to be wondered at that, with three such humorously grim experiences, I begin to fight somewhat shy of participating in Festivals for the future?

12

TRADITION, STYLE AND THE
THEATRE TODAY

TRADITION, ACCORDING to the dictionary, is 'the handing down of customs, opinions or doctrines from ancestors to posterity, from the past to the present, by oral communication: an opinion, custom or doctrine thus handed down: principles or accumulated experiences of earlier generations handed on to others.'

It is often said that the English stage has none of the great tradition of acting which has given dignity and substance to the theatres of France, Germany and Russia in their finest days. The National Theatre, we are told, will create a similar tradition in England, a permanent company for acting classic plays with style. Style (I quote again from the dictionary) is 'the general formal characteristics of any fine art'. A broad generalization, surely, and not a particularly illuminating definition. What exactly is style in acting and stage production? Does it mean the correct wearing of costume, appropriate deportment and the 'nice conduct of a clouded cane'? Does it also imply a correct interpretation of the text, without undue exaggeration or eccentricity, an elegant sense of period, and beautiful unselfconscious speaking by a balanced and versatile company of players, used to working together; flexible instruments under the hand of an inspired director? Such were the theatres of

Stanislavsky in Russia, Copeau in France, and during certain years, of Reinhardt's supremacy in Germany.

An individual actor can have style. A production can achieve a general style. And this word 'style' can apply equally to a modern play or a costume piece, to comedy and tragedy alike.

It is a doubtful question whether tradition and style can be studied and learnt in a dramatic school, or acquired by watching good acting, or by reading accounts of the famous performances given by great players of the past. Every year students flock to the Old Vic and Stratford-on-Avon from many parts of the world (and especially from America) to learn 'the way to act Shakespeare'. It would be interesting to know what conclusions they carry away with them. For the glamour and past traditions of the English theatre merge so imperceptibly into the theatre we know today that it is hard to know which of the two influences is the stronger.

Some actors and directors try to escape altogether from the web of tradition, especially in the best known Shakespearian plays and parts. Too often in the last twenty years they have achieved originality at the expense of the plays themselves. The actors who try to play Shakespeare dressed in clothes of some other period – Macbeth in Byronic costume, Rosalind as a Watteau lady – are encumbered, and not only by their clothes. They have to play in the manner of one period as regards deportment and behaviour while interpreting a character conceived and written in another. Shakespeare has already confused the issue with his own anachronisms, and too much modern ingenuity in decorating his plays will only add to the confusion. Granville-Barker has of course suggested that some of the plays should be staged with Renaissance-classical costumes, in the manner of Paolo Veronese and Tintoretto, and this legitimate experiment has been tried with varying success, most happily in the obviously appropriate case of *Antony and Cleopatra*,[1] to which it is particularly suited.

But style in acting does not consist solely of the external elegances.

What are the most important qualities for a classical actor? Imagination, sensibility and power. Relaxation, repose and the art of listening. To speak well and move gracefully, these are elementary feats which can be mastered with hard work and practice, though some great actors, Irving in particular, seem occasionally to have succeeded without them. The young actor, if he has a love of tradition and a natural respect for experience, may be inclined at first to prefer to try and imitate the less subtle excellences of other actors he has seen. His own taste may not be good. But, as he grows older, he will be increasingly influenced by the pictures he sees, the books he reads, the music he hears and the experiences of his own life, rather than by the acting of other players, trusting more confidently to his own instinct and personal discoveries about human character and emotions. His own experience of acting in several different kinds of plays will teach him much, of course, and often a fine actor of modern parts, who plays for the first time in a classical play, may bring a far truer sense of style to his performance than an actor who is steeped in tradition and can boast of a long career in Shakespeare.

As he grows in experience and power, the actor discovers that the make-believe side of acting is not sufficient, unless it is also founded on a personal admission of self-revelation. At first he may enjoy, as children do, pretending, dressing up in order to

---

[1] Old Vic & Sadlers Wells 1930: John Gielgud and Dorothy Green.
Piccadilly Theatre 1946: Godfrey Tearle and Edith Evans.
Stratford-on-Avon 1953: Michael Redgrave and Peggy Ashcroft.

look and behave like someone else. But he will soon find that in impersonating a character like Macbeth, however well he may simulate the externals of the part – the age, deportment and physical aspects of his impersonation – he must also find his own personal reactions to the speeches and situations with absolute truth. Now as he can only execute the promptings of his imagination within the limits of his own technical instrument and range of personality, he must discover for himself what he, and he alone, can do to bring the character to the stage in his own individual way. And here Shakespeare provides wonderfully for the actor. For in his great characters there is such a wide sweep of creation, so many subtle varieties of colour, that a dozen actors may choose a dozen ways of playing them.

Tradition can only be handed down, a delightful but ephemeral mixture of legend, history and hearsay, but style evolves afresh through the finest talents of each succeeding generation, influencing, in its own particular era, the quality both of acting and of production. The theatre needs both, and thrives on both, for both are the result of discipline, of endless experiment, trial and error, of individual brilliance and devotion. And genius may always be relied on to appear suddenly from nowhere, breaking all rules and confounding all theory by sheer magnetism and originality.

Can we ever achieve a permanent classical company in England? Granville-Barker attempted it, made one or two brilliant starts, and foundered with the first world war. Nigel Playfair and J. B. Fagan profited from his experience, and (to a limited extent) created theatres of their own with integrity and style, using a nucleus of actors and actresses whose early training under the actor-manager stars, Tree, Benson, Alexander and others, had already developed their talents to a point when they were well fitted to become members of a company where the policy was bent towards interpreting good team plays without sacrificing their balance. Our so-called character actors are surely as fine as any in the world and, as the body of every repertory company, they are, of course, essential. They are versatile and loyal. But, curiously enough, they seem to do their best work under an autocrat – whether he be actor, director, or a combination of both. For it is the leaders of such companies who create their own tradition of style and ensemble playing. But soon they have to face the fact that the more brilliant among the younger members begin to find themselves cramped, and so feel bound to break away from the nursery, to become leading actors in their turn, and inaugurate a new tradition of their own. So it happened with Mrs Kendal, with Ellen Terry, with Irving, Forbes-Robertson, Tree, Alexander and Granville-Barker, and in our own day with Sybil Thorndike, Edith Evans, Peggy Ashcroft, Ralph Richardson, Laurence Olivier, Alec Guinness, Paul Scofield and myself.

The struggle is always the same. Between the star actor's personal magnetism, the public's demand for outstanding personalities, and the author's dependence on them to interpret the leading roles in their plays, and that ideal theatre in which author, designer, actors and director are all bent together to contrive an unselfish, perfectly balanced creation in which no part shall be greater than the whole.

It is evident that the star must always exist. Is he to sacrifice his choice of parts and the development of his personal career to the establishment of a theatre of which he is the head? If so, he must stand down in certain productions, and either play a small part, or direct, or not appear at all. But in that case he must have in his company one or two actors with talent and drawing-power equal to his own – a very difficult achievement, since star actors are comparatively few and always greatly in demand. In addition, he must guarantee his company long-term engagements – but not so long that they will become exhausted and dissatisfied. Also his actors must agree not to accept film and radio work, since they will be required to rehearse continually; and sufficiently attractive parts must be provided for each player – at least one good part in a season, say, of four plays. Experimental plays must be alternated with some of the well-known classics which are most certain to attract the public, but the modern authors must accept a ready-made cast (which may imperil the chances of their work, since in a repertory company a certain amount of less-than-perfect casting is inevitable) as well as a limited run. Yet it is essential that a classical company should sometimes work on an original modern script, even though a Shakespearian team is seldom well suited for a modern play, in which women are so often more predominant and there are seldom enough parts to accommodate a very large company. If actors are laid off for a certain play (which may be an admirable respite for them), they must be paid during their holiday time or they will go and work elsewhere. Economically, as well as artistically, the prospect is a bleak one; and it seems to me remarkable that, with the interruption of two world wars, the advent of films, radio and television, and the enormous rise in expenses in every department of the theatre – all these crises following one another in rapid succession – the experiments in classic repertory and semi-permanent companies made during the last thirty years have succeeded at all.

But the struggle is unending. It seems sad, of course, that when at long last a really fine production is achieved, it cannot be kept in the repertoire of the theatre which has created it, to be revived at intervals over several years, and shown in America and the great capitals of Europe too. But that is the glory of the theatre as well as its fallibility. Talented players develop quickly, and cannot be kept in subordinate positions for long. The best ensemble will deteriorate after a hundred performances of the same play. Actors cannot work together happily for too many years at a time. Directors become stale. Style changes. Stars become too old to wish to continue playing the great parts in which they made their reputation a few years ago (this was not always so, and surely is a sign of grace among the players of today).

The repertory theatre and the classical theatre must always be the best nurseries. They will attract talented young people who wish to learn their craft, and a few of the best established stars and character actors will always be glad to work in them too – but only for a limited period, for the work is intensely concentrated and demanding, and the rewards financially inferior. In addition there are the purely material considerations to discourage the fine non-star actor who is no longer young – continuous rehearsals and learning of new parts, sharing of dressing-rooms, unfeatured billing, and the binding terms of a long contract.

Practical men of vision are rare in the theatre. It is seldom that one man can combine the talents of impresario, financial manager, director and actor. He may have a smattering of all these qualifications but, if so, he is best fitted to work in a theatre building which belongs to him, and to devise his own policy for running it. He will hardly be likely to work so well under a committee or a board of governors, however indulgent. But if he works alone as an autocrat, makes wrong decisions, or becomes tired or ill after a concentrated period of hard work, his theatre will collapse as Irving's did in the end. Under present-day conditions there is little possibility that he can back his own ventures, so that he is bound to be financially responsible to a patron or syndicate, or else he must work, under someone else's management, in whatever theatre that management is able to provide for him and to some degree, therefore, under the supervision of others. The conditions cannot be ideal, however one looks at them. The demand is always far greater than the supply as far as talent is concerned – and the temperament of theatre people notoriously incalculable. Actors are nearly always wonderfully loyal in adversity, and sometimes strangely difficult when things are going well.

But there is a great new public for the theatre since the last war. The little clique of middle-class theatre-lovers of the Victorian and Edwardian times is gone for ever. They were regular and critical playgoers, inclined to be conventionally-minded, following the favourite authors and players of their day, fearful of experiment and suspicious of innovation. They loved Shakespeare chiefly as a stamping-ground for stars and spectacle, and revelled in the melodramas which the cinema has now usurped for ever. Today books are more widely read, films and radio have increased the public demand for entertainment, and an appetite for literature, acting, and the spoken word has spread to millions of potential playgoers who would never have dreamed of entering a theatre forty years ago. Plays are read, listened to and discussed as well as seen. There is a much wider interest in the production of intelligent new work. Criticism is more general, if often less well informed and expert. And though one may venture to resent pipes being smoked, evening papers being read, and open-necked shirts being worn in the stalls of a theatre, the audience of today is really far more widely representative than the snobbish, socially divided public of our parents' day.

Audiences are still traditionally-minded. They are ready to applaud as a general rule, and to hiss occasionally, though a good deal less frequently than of old. They still stand in queues, arrive late, drop tea-trays, and hover at stage-doors.

Behind the curtain too, a good deal of old tradition remains, as much an inevitable part of the theatre magic as the plush curtains, the jumbled property-room, the narrow bleak passages and staircases where the actors pass, now in costume, now in their street clothes, and the dressing-rooms with their pinned-up yellowing telegrams, strangely assorted mascots, and reminders scribbled in grease-paint across the mirrors. And yet tradition is not a god that should be worshipped in the theatre. It encourages a sentimental looking-backward. It is a warning as well as an example, a danger as well as an ideal.

13

ACTORS AND AUDIENCES

TO THE YOUNG ACTOR

ACTING IS A flexible contributory form of art, depending as it does on the fusion of author, director and a mixed team of personalities working on a text. In the finest performances it is impossible to perceive where the craftsmanship leaves off and the art begins. But all actors must begin somehow to learn their craft and find their own individual rules for practising and developing it to the best advantage.

There are certain hints and guideposts therefore that may perhaps be useful to beginners, and that may help them to enter the theatre with a sense of discipline and to experiment constructively in the right direction.

First, I would say, you must learn to become a good partner. Just as in a game you are a member of a team, so on the stage you must try to provide the right support, balance and background. Learn how to listen. Remember that when you stop speaking yourself another player has to continue, and that he relies, in picking up his cue, on the tone and pace you have established before him. Be serious, devoted and disciplined, but do not take yourself too seriously. Nothing is more tiresome than the actor who pesters his colleagues with his own personal problems and theories about acting. Develop a thick skin for listening to adverse criticism, and a tolerance of your colleagues, even when you feel sure they may be in the wrong. It is better to keep your theories about acting to yourself, but if you must discuss them with someone, choose the right moment for asking the director, preferably when he is not actively engaged in his own complicated work. If you are in a long run, try to experiment continually without spoiling other people's effects or diverging from the main pattern originally rehearsed by the director. Develop your sensitivity, try to observe and correct your personal mannerisms, be exact in your diction, gesture and movement. Above all remember that your voice, the chief instrument of your craft, can be capable of infinite subtleties of tone, pace and rhythm, and must not be exaggerated or flattened out under the strain of constant repetition. Carry your lines through to the ends of sentences; do not pounce on your cues with over-emphasis; remember the final consonants, avoid dropping your voice at the end of a line.

Build your character at rehearsals from within and, when you are learning your lines, take care to memorize them, not parrot-wise, but in relation to the balance and progression of the scene, and in collaboration with the director and your fellow actors.

In playing a love scene, learn to show off your partner rather than trying to exhibit yourself. Just as in ballet the woman is shown to her greatest advantage by the strength and self-effacing support of her male partner, so in a play the woman relies upon the man to provide her with the background against which she can most skilfully create her infinite variety of mood and grace.

Lastly, and most important of all I would say, try to discover the secret to the difficult art of relaxation. Husband your emotional resources, select your moments of climax so as to gain real power and range. Once you have acquired confidence on the one hand and relaxation on the other, you will at last begin to progress to a more creative skill by developing the originality and selectiveness which are the hall-marks of the true artist.

SERVANTS OF THE PUBLIC

'What kind of audience tonight?' the actors say to one another as they stand in the wings waiting for their entrances. It would perhaps be more to the purpose if they said, 'What kind of performance are we giving tonight?' Yet surely it is a very natural anxiety on the actor's part, this childish anxiety to provoke the response he longs for, that warm sympathetic appreciation which enables him to relax on the stage and transform his labours into love.

The first night of a new play, agonizing though it must always be for the sensitive player, does at least arouse in a company of actors a feeling of unselfishness. They are drawn together in the service of the play, regardless of the recognition each may hope to gain by his individual performance.

How much should players allow an audience to affect them? Some will tell you they love rehearsals but despair once the early performances are past, wearily sinking into a daily mono-tony of repetition which forces them to elaborate or become perfunctory till they finally lose interest altogether. Others delight unashamedly in the laughter and tears they evoke. Others again act more consciously to please the public than they do to serve the play by collaborating unselfishly with their fellows.

Some of the finest actors I know refuse to discuss the quality of an audience, at least while the performance is in progress. This refusal, which surprised me at first, now strikes me as a fine example, for discipline in a company is always greatly affected by the behaviour of the leading players, and it is inspiring to work with an artist of outstanding talent who is also unselfish, courteous and punctual, and who checks or spurs himself and everyone else when the play seems to be going slackly, instead of blaming the audience for apathy, as so many of us are apt to do.

It is perhaps more the business of the director than of the actor to study audiences closely. On the other hand, the better the actor, the more certain is he of his own skill and power to control his audience. So he may, according to his temperament, be permitted a certain elasticity of performance, not only because his task in a complicated role is an excessively arduous and exacting one, but also because his variations can help to quicken, not only his own spontaneity, but that of his fellow actors, who must sustain a receptive and lively reaction in order to keep up with him if he changes his pace and detail. He must not be tempted, however, to 'run away with the play', and to destroy the ensemble for the sake of original and selfish improvisations which may ruin the intentions of the author and director.

Audiences pay to see great acting even more readily than to see a great play, and will always reserve their warmest affection for a player of outstanding quality, whatever vehicle he may choose in which to exhibit his talents. A fine actor may often have poor taste, and genuinely prefer a second-rate, showy text to a first-rate one. It is often a temptation to an actor to 'play safe' by appearing in the kind of plays which have always seemed to bring him the greatest fame and popularity in his most successful days. Experimental work in the theatre, if unappreciated, can break an artist's heart as well as ruin his pocket. Poel, Granville-Barker, Gordon Craig, all these men have been greater influences on the theatre today than they were thought to be when they were struggling to assert themselves in London years ago. But an actor who experiments risks his personal popularity more than a director does, and both may find it hard to make a living. The actor, however powerful his originality, must always remain the servant of the public before whom he does his work.

I do not believe theatre audiences have greatly changed in quality in the last few years, though in all parts of the house they represent a more varied section of the community than the small, well-fed, well-dressed coterie of theatre-goers who filled the stalls and dress-circle in days gone by. The two wars created an appetite for 'entertainment', and the phrase, 'Let's go to a show', which would have horrified our grandparents (and the old actors), is not so depressingly indiscriminate as one might at first suppose. Good new plays find their audience in a surprisingly short space of time; bad, careless work is still rightly censured; the occupants of the less expensive seats still endure the discomforts and drawbacks of indifferent sight and sound, and pass judgement on a first night with the old traditional signs of enthusiasm or displeasure.

CRITICS

The critic, one imagines, anticipates going to the theatre as apprehensively as the average actor when he wakes up on a matinée day. On a first night, the tremors which send alternate waves of despair and hope round the dressing-rooms, to say nothing of the feelings of anticipation among the paying audience, affect him not at all. While he watches and listens, he must distinguish dispassionately between intention and achievement. He is unlikely to be swayed by the audience's contribution and reaction to the evening's entertainment and, whatever he may write later in his notice, he may be sure he will not please the actors. Even when he gives praise, they are disappointed to find that he has missed entirely what they consider to be some obvious point of excellence in their performance, and if he writes adversely they decide that he is unfair (or has dined unwisely) belittling honest effort and perhaps ruining the chances of a new author or an enterprising management.

Actors love to read good notices, of course, though personally I am always inclined myself to be suspicious of praise (however much I like to read it) and perhaps tend to be over-impressed by a bad review. It is sometimes helpful to be shown one's faults, though personal attacks, especially on physical defects or mannerisms (even if one knows them to be true) can be cruelly wounding, and make one self-conscious for a long time afterwards.

Some actors do not read their notices, at least not until several weeks after a first night, when their emotional reactions have become less vulnerable. I wish I was strong-minded enough to follow their example. How far should one take heed of other people's opinions, critics, friends and colleagues? The letters from members of the audience who write complaining that they could not hear can hardly fail to disturb one's self-complacency. These critics at least have a legitimate and practical grievance. Most of us have one or two trusted friends with whom we can discuss our acting problems and whose opinion we respect, especially if they are not too much prejudiced in our favour. It seems inadvisable to me for actors and professional critics to foregather off the stage. It is extremely difficult for both sides to preserve an impartial attitude to one another, and a carefully guarded conversation is very rarely satisfactory. The critic may take advantage of the fact that his written account of contemporary acting may influence the opinion of future generations. This, after all, has already happened in the case of Hazlitt and other great critics of the past. The actor, knowing this, may resent the fact that his skill and talent may very well be disparaged or overlooked, and that this will misrepresent him to posterity in print. But does what is said or written about them really matter very much to players after they are dead? The critic may be able to record a moment of magic, may describe some piece of business, some cry of emotion, with a vivid phrase of re-creation. Then, too, there are tapes, recordings, films, to preserve our voices and faces as never before, although we can hardly fail to be well aware that these mechanical devices may easily expose our work to ridicule for the ears and eyes of a later generation.

But nothing can compare with the magic of the real occasion, which is to me the true glory of the ephemeral art of the theatre – the living actor appearing before the living audience; the silence, the tension, the entrances and exits, the laughter and applause, the subtle changes between one night's performance and another's. The thrill of success, the dread of monotony, the pride of discipline; the impatient drudgery of repetition, the bitterness of failure, the sense of eternal imperfection, with its occasional reward in a moment or two of thrilling contact with a particularly responsive audience. This is the actor's unique personal achievement, rewarding him, for just a few short minutes, for all the experiments and labours and disappointments of many years.

APPENDIX 1

After the death of Granville-Barker in 1946 I searched in vain for my rehearsal copy of *King Lear* in which I had hastily scribbled many of his hints on tone, motives and technical delivery of lines. Shortly before beginning to study the play again for Stratford-on-Avon in 1950, I was lucky enough to find the missing copy in a neglected corner of a drawer. Here are the majority of the notes. I add them in the hope that they may bring to others (as they do so vividly to me) an echo of the exactness which Barker showed in his criticism and guidance, and his understanding of every mood and nuance in the part of Lear. Here are the notes exactly as I scribbled them down at the time.[1]

ACT I. SCENE I

[Lear enters ceremoniously from the side carrying a huge staff which he uses to walk with. Reaching the centre of the stage, on his way to the throne, which commands the stage up centre, he suddenly stops, and striking the staff impatiently on the floor, raps out his first command to Gloucester – then he gives the staff to an attendant and mounts the throne. Pleased. Happy.]

[1] These notes were recorded by Sir John in his copy of the play – an edition now no longer available. The line numbers here given refer to Professor Sisson's edition of *The Complete Works of William Shakespeare* (Odhams, London 1954). There are slight differences between the edition used by Barker and Professor Sisson's, but it was thought advantageous to leave the line as studied by the actor.

Line

102   *Nothing will come of nothing.*   First note of danger.

106   *How now, Cordelia, mend your speech a little.*   Grind. Intimidation.

124   *By the sacred radiance of the sun.*   Big without ponging (actor's slang for hamming).

131-2 *The barbarous Scythian.*   Oath over, sulk over this. Descending passage.

139   *I loved her most.*   Justify himself.

152   *With reservation of an hundred knights.*   He thinks this disposes of the whole thing, lean back, happy as at opening.

178   *Kent, on thy life, no more.*   Dead quiet. Turn. Stare at him.

197   *Since thou hast sought to make us break our vow.*   Everyone must listen. Write this down.

205   *If on the tenth day following.* – Get a note of this (to secretary).

[After exit of Kent.]   Lear – complete change – smooth, courtly, charming, anger vanished.

[To Burgundy.]   Irony, smooth, cruel about Cordelia, urbanity, very ironic, schoolmaster showing up dunce.

[To France (whom he liked).]   More respect, genuine. Don't look at Cordelia again.

289   *Nothing. I have sworn, I am firm.*   Real, sulky. Big Ben striking. Pass by exit, cut her dead.

515   *The jewels of our father with washed eyes.*   Cordelia weeps *not* for the behaviour of Lear, but because of the kindness of France in accepting her.

ACT I. SCENE IV

[With Kent in disguise. Robust, jolly, give and take, enjoy sparring. Sing, genial, throw things about (gloves, whip, etc.). Boots off, shoes on, nuisance. Suddenly checked by the insolence of the knight, continue gloves, etc., mechanically, sudden stop.]

68   *Thou but rememberest me of mine own conception.*   I saw it, felt it, can't be really so.

Line

85   *Do you bandy looks*   Take cloth from table, strike him across
      with me?   the face. Stand quite still, hands on hips.
                      Terrific. Kent trips Oswald. Roars with
                      laughter.

[At entrance of Fool.] Sit him by me, give him food. Immensely
fond, sweet to him. Eat and drink heartily. Show him off to
Kent.

112 *Take heed sirrah, the whip.*   Not too fast. Encourage Fool to go
                         on, buy it. This will be a good one
                         I expect.

No welcome from Goneril. Suddenly notices her. Take it in.

225 *Are you our daughter?*   Blank.

232 *Does any here know me?*   Danger – end of careless exterior.
                       Gasps. Feeling. Speech nothing.

243 *Your name, fair gentlewoman.*   Bite. During her speech store
                       it up – hold back.

262 *Darkness and Devils.*   Crash. Pause between sentences.
[Entrance of Albany.]   More reason. Down towards her. See
                      her. Find it.

285 *Oh, Lear, Lear, Lear.*   Let go. The curse sudden, surprise the
                      audience.
                      Speak nicely to Albany, going, then
                      down to her. Strange, not loud.
                      Deadly. Ride it.

304 *Sharper than a serpent's tooth.*   Climax. Move backwards
                       from her.

305 *Away, away.*   Will not go back on it. Slow exit.
[Sudden   Broken speech in contrast to former scene.
reappearance.]   Change after 'What's the matter sir?' See
            Goneril. Burst into tears. Not too much. Not
            repeat the curse.

ACT I. SCENE V

[Represents the journey from Goneril's castle to Gloster's.]
[At entrance.]   Touch of the ruler. Characteristic. Quick, not
           thinking of what he says. Walks continually to
           and fro. Stop suddenly – deep walk *I did her*
           wrong stop again.

Line

33/4   *Be my horses ready?*   Shout. Move about.

38   *Because they are not eight?*   Angry. Heard it before.

40   *Monster ingratitude.* Walk again.

43   *How's that?*   Sudden.

46   *O let me not be mad.*   Now afraid *inside*. Simple.

50   *Come boy.* Sustained exit. Use Fool as focal point in the scene throughout.

ACT II. SCENE IV

[Arrival at Gloster's Castle.] Pace at which you left. Start again.

[At entrance.] Puzzled but confident.

7   *Ha?* Turn. Very slow, very outraged.

15   *What's he that hath so much thy place mistook?*   Deadly. Exchange with Kent in the stocks. Pride hurt. Superb.

25   *Thou durst not do it.*   Slow rhythm. Dignity offended. Too indignant to be angry.

[During Kent's speech.] Absorb the insult.

118/9   *My breath and blood.*   Recover, then hysteria again.

123   *We are not ourselves.*   (As he felt just now himself.)

128   *Death on my state.*   Sudden rage.

133   *Duke and's wife.*   More than temper.

136   *I'll beat the drum.*   Deepest round this point.

139   *O me, my heart.*   Physical. Entirely new voice. Quick. Then stand still. Pay no attention to the Fool. Closed eyes, hand to head.

Entrance of Cornwall and Regan. Begin right down.

145   *Good morrow to you both.*   No greeting. Cold.

147   *I am glad to see your highness.*   Don't notice this.

148   *Regan I think you are.*   Tender, just. (In his heart he knows.)

156/7   *Thou'lt not believe with how depraved a quality.*   Literal.

161   *Say how is that?*   Stern, suspicious.

167   *My curses on her.*   Then control it.

182   *Never, Regan.*   Definite. Then a bit petty and distracted, not deliberate.

190   *You nimble lightnings.*   Rash mood. Burble.

Line

196   *No Regan thou shalt never have my curse.*   Exhausted by the rage. Tender silly.

200   *'Tis not in thee.*   Fear that he may be wrong. (You didn't mean it, did you?)

      [Does not take in Goneril's arrival till her appearance, turns to door, and sees her suddenly. Then sees Kent too again.]

210   *Who put my man i' the stocks?*   King.

221   *Who comes here? O heavens.*   Knowledge gradually growing, more moved than ever.

222   *If you do love old men?*   Noble, becoming helpless.

228   *O Regan, wilt thou take her by the hand?*   Dignity. Slow.

237   *You! Did you?*   Utter Contempt. Period.

249   *The hot-blooded France that dowerless took our youngest born.*   Paint it, then off again.

253   *Slave and sumpter.*   Preposterous.

256   *I prithee daughter do not make me mad.*   Physical. Real. Turn swift.

260   *Or rather a disease that's in my flesh.*   Rash mood. Then suffer in the head.

292   *I gave you all.*   Very big. To the front. Bewildered. Not as fast as their speeches.

299   *These wicked creatures yet do look well-favour'd.*   (Goneril better than Regan.) Tremble.

310   *O reason not the need.*   Drop it right down. Ironic feeling. Dignity.

320   *You see me here, you gods.*   Sink on to bench. Simple. Crouching attitude.

326   *Stain my man's cheeks.*   Collapse here. Rash mood suddenly. Human, broken old man, futile. Suddenly looks at them. Wipe eyes. Then up and totter off but more firmly at the end for the horses.

      Self-devouring rages. Physical symptoms which he ignores.

ACT III.   SCENE II [1st *Storm Scene*]

    Tune in. Pitch voice. Low key. Oratorio. Every word impersonal.

Line

21 *Here I stand, your slave.* Simpler. Voice down, then up. Keep still. Feet.

54 *Let the great gods.* Full value. Point to the audience.

66/7 *I am a man more sinn'd against than sinning.* Simple. Clasp head.

[GOING MAD]

87 *My wits begin to turn.* Real not pitiful.

89 *Where is this straw my fellow.* Kind, next lines casual, make little of them.

Listen tenderly to the Fool, cloak round him (*how nicely you sing*). Hold on to the edge of security. Leave stage on a high, unfinished note.

ACT III. SCENE IV [*2nd Heath scene*]

MAD now. Strange Walk. Strange Voice. Living in purely metaphysical world. At entrance. Distant, dignified.

17 *The tempest in my mind.* Point to head. Move away from them all. Words tumbling out.

24 *O Regan, Goneril.* Climax. See it all in a circle. Vision.

27 *O, that way madness lies.* Horror. Then drop it.

30 *Prithee, go in thyself.* Kind. Stoop to touch the Fool.

34 *I'll pray (and when I have prayed) then I'll sleep.* Away to thought. Kneel in mire. Hands folded conventionally.

The Fool's scream turns him off his head. Leans back on knees. Look through cage – fingers in front of face.

57 *Didst thou give all to thy daughter.* Is that all? Face each other. Still.

72 *Have his daughters brought him to this pass.* Sad dignity. Pity now new.

78 *Now all the plagues.* Just *too* dignified. (Explain to me.)

87 *Judicious punishment.* (Quite right.)

97 *What hast thou been?* Too interested. Listen to his answer and nod approval.

[126]

Line

115 *Why thou wert better in thy grave.* Speak to no one. Full value. Now faster.

123 *Off you lendings.* Rash mood suddenly back. Afterward slow, still, stare vacantly.

139 *How fares your grace?* Curious silence.
After Gloster enters. Still Important. King. Walk round stage with Edgar talking to him.

171 *First let me talk with this philosopher.* Wave Gloster aside. Keep step with Edgar.
Fantastic bowing and pantomime.

199 *Come, let's in all.* Still grand.

207 *Come, good Athenian.* Very courteous. Get him again by the arm.
At the end of scene, nod in approval, march off in same rhythm as we walked before.

ACT III. SCENE VI [*Hovel*]
Very odd and mysterious. Gradual disintegration.

11 *A King. A King.* Indignant.

20 *It shall be done.* Action does not begin till here. Firm. Sudden move. Swinging stool in hand.

31 *The foul fiend haunts poor Tom.* Stand aghast. Lunatic for the first time. Paler and paler in voice.

37 *I'll see their trial first.* Stop them dancing.

40 *You are o' the commission.* Bow, conduct him to place. He is counsel for the prosecution.

53 *She cannot deny it.* Very reasonable.

60 *Why hast thou let her 'scape?* Tiny, trembling, old man, childlike, tottering about.

66 *The little dogs and all.* Piteous. In Kent's arms.
Equal value to real and imagined characters, whole scene QUIET.

84/5 *You, sir, I entertain you for one* Exhausted courtesy to Edgar.
of my hundred.

Sink onto bench. Lie down. Poke head out again between imaginary curtains. Then lie again hand under cheek.

[127]

ACT IV. SCENE VI [*Dover Cliff*]

Happy King of Nature. No troubles. Tremendously dignified. Branch in hand, like staff in opening scene, walk with it.

Line

113 *Give the word.*   Nice. Applaud Edgar as he says 'Pass'.

117 *Ha! Goneril with a white beard.*   Frightful pain. Rub head.

125 *Go to, they are not men o' their word.*   Sad. All away from the others but don't move about.

130 *Ay, every inch a King.*   Direct answer, change from sad mood.

134 *Die for adultery? No.*   Light.

137 *Let Copulation thrive.*   Almost jolly. Swing staff above head.

137 *For Gloster's bastard son.*   Special.

141 *To't Luxury, pell mell.*   Comedy.

142 *Behold yond simpering dame.*   Horrid.

146 *The fitchew nor the soiled horse.*   Words.

148 *Down from the waist.*   Intimate. Quicker. Build speech.

159 *Let me wipe it first.*   Real. Physical. Comfortable with Gloster.

163 *Do thy worst blind Cupid.*   Coy. Then different key, tone, pace.

169 *Read.*   Very cross.

172/3 *Your eyes are in a heavy case.*   Joke.

186 *Thou rascal Beadle.*   Vision. Begin to get excited. Quicker. Bursts of feeling. Flow on.

199 *Get thee glass eyes.*   A bit impatient with him. After boots are off, sudden relief. Recognize Gloster slowly, comforting him (*I will preach to thee*).

212 *When we are born.*   Serio-comic.

213 *This, a good block.*   Very light.

217 *Kill, kill.*   Build to revenge. End of scene for feeling.

220 *No rescue what! A prisoner?*   Panic. Then light, helpless.

226 *This would make a man a man of salt.*   Empty chatter.

ACT IV. SCENE VII [*Awakening*]

Sit in profile in chair. Hands in lap. Make them up again.

55 *You do me wrong.*   A bit sulky.

60 *You are a spirit I know.*   Puzzled.

[128]

Line
62 *Where have I been?* Real. Don't anticipate.
64 *I should even die with pity.* A bit cross.
68/69 *Would I were assured of my condition.* Troubled. Keep it up.
     Not conscious of surroundings.
87 *Be your tears wet?* Lift her head. ⎫ He hears the voice he
                                        ⎪ knows, but fears so
95 *Do not abuse me.* Strong.   ⎬ terribly she may not be
                                        ⎪ Cordelia.
                                        ⎭
102 *You must bear with me.* Cheerful. End. Come off it.
     Rise as if from throne. Soft dignity at exit.

ACT V. SCENE III [*Going to prison*]
10 *Come let's away to prison.* Delighted. Really happy. Dance
                                  the whole speech like a polka.
                                  Music up and down. Variety.
     Exit hand in hand with her, triumphant.

ACT V. SCENE III [*Death*]
308 *Howl, howl.* Take time. Dreadful.
308 *O you are men of stone.* Anger. Hold them off.
328 *Prithee away.* Strong.
331 *I killed the slave.* (You know.)
334 *I have seen the day.* Jolly. Stand firm above her body.
336 *I am old now.* Sudden break.
     Forget Cordelia in passage with Kent.
345/6 *He's dead and rotten.* Suddenly sad.
351 *You are welcome hither.* Careless. Shake hands. Move
                               away. Wander about at back of
                               stage.
     Find the body again. The rope round her neck.
     Crouch by her. Kneel.
375 *Pray you, undo this button.* Real, then a cry.
376 *Look on her.* Joy.

LETTERS FROM GRANVILLE-BARKER TO JOHN GIELGUD
ON KING LEAR

The Athenaeum,
Pall Mall, S.W.1.

Sunday morning
[April 14, 1940]

My dear Gielgud. Lear is in your grasp.

Forget all the things I have bothered you about. Let your own now well self-disciplined instincts carry you along, and up; simply allowing the checks and changes to prevent your being carried *away*. And I prophesy – happily – great things for you.

Yrs.
H.G.B.

May 6th 1940
18 Place des Etats-Unis.

My dear Gielgud. Your letter of the 2nd arrived this morning.
I'll take thought and answer it tomorrow.

Meanwhile here's a trifling point:

In the last scene Lear quite ignores (as you now do) the 'Tis noble
Kent, your friend' and merely gives a general answer 'A plague upon
you, murderers, traitors all.' And later when he looks at him and
says 'Are you not Kent?' it should clearly be in a highly indignant
'How-dare-you-enter-our-presence-after-I-have-banished-you'
tone. And when Kent answers 'The same, your servant Kent' before
he can go on to the rest of the line, the old gentleman should repeat,
rather feebly, the magnificent 'out of my sight' gesture with which
in the first scene he banished him. '*He*'s a good fellow – *He*'ll
strike . . .' clearly refers to the Caius impersonation and the tripping
up and beating of Oswald. Perhaps we did work this out.

Yrs.
H.G.B.

April 29, [1940]
18, Place des Etats-Unis.

My dear Gielgud. Did we ever agree as to the precise moment at which Lear goes off his head?

I believe that Poor Tom's appearance from the hovel marks it. The 'grumbling' inside, the Fool's scream of terror, the wild figure suddenly appearing – that combination would be enough to send him over the border-line. Do you mark the moment by doing something quite *new*? Difficult, I know, to find anything new to do at that moment. But something queer and significant of madness, followed (it would help) by a dead silence, before you say (again in a voice you have not used before)

Didst thou give all . . .

I don't doubt you have devised something. But thinking over the scene this struck me – ought to have struck me before; perhaps we *did* agree to it – so I drop you this line.

You're having an interesting, if exhausting, time, I am sure, and I fancy a most successful one. Congratulations.

Yrs.
H.G.B.

From H. Granville-Barker
To   John Gielgud

April 30, morning.
I think I have it: –
see next sheet.

. . . shows the heavens more just.
> Lear remains on knees at end of prayer, head buried
> in hands.

Edg: *Father . . . poor Tom.*

make much of this; don't hurry it; give it a 'Banshee'
effect, lilt and rhythm.
At the sound Lear lifts his head. Face seen through his
outspread fingers (suggestion of madman looking
through bars).
The Fool screams and runs on: business as at present.
This gets Lear to his feet. He turns towards the hovel
watching intently for what will emerge.

Dialogue as at present.

Edgar's entrance and speech: *Away . . . warm thee,*
much as now. And Lear immensely struck by it. cf.
Hamlet-Ghost. Just as it is finishing (Edg. not to hurry
it) stalk him to present position for *Didst thou . . .*

and, as he turns for the speech, at B, we see that he is
now quite off his head.

N.B. Once Edgar is on, he Kent and Fool must keep
deadly still so that these movements of Lear may have
their effect. Translate the Hamlet-Ghost business into
terms of Lear and it will about give you the effect.

I believe this may be right. Worth trying anyhow.

APPENDIX 2

MERCHANT OF VENICE	(1932)	The Old Vic, London. Peggy Ashcroft, Malcolm Keen.
	(1938)	Queen's Theatre, London. Peggy Ashcroft, John Gielgud.
HAMLET	(1934)	New Theatre, London. Laura Cowie, Jessica Tandy, Frank Vosper, John Gielgud.
	(1939)	Lyceum Theatre, London. Fay Compton, Laura Cowie, Jack Hawkins, John Gielgud.
ROMEO AND JULIET	(1932)	The O.U.D.S., Oxford. Edith Evans, Peggy Ashcroft.
	(1935)	New Theatre, London. Edith Evans, Peggy Ashcroft. Laurence Olivier and John Gielgud alternated in the parts of Romeo and Mercutio.
MACBETH	(1942)	Piccadilly Theatre, London. Gwen Ffrangcon-Davies, John Gielgud.
	(1954)	Memorial Theatre, Stratford-on-Avon. Margaret Leighton, Ralph Richardson.

MUCH ADO ABOUT NOTHING	(1949)	Memorial Theatre, Stratford-on-Avon. Diana Wynyard, Anthony Quayle.
	(1952)	Phoenix Theatre, London. Peggy Ashcroft, John Gielgud.
	(1955)	Palace Theatre, London. Peggy Ashcroft, John Gielgud.
	(1959)	New York, U.S.A. Margaret Leighton, John Gielgud.
TWELFTH NIGHT	(1955)	Memorial Theatre, Stratford-on-Avon. Vivien Leigh, Laurence Olivier.
KING LEAR	(1950)	Memorial Theatre, Stratford-on-Avon. Peggy Ashcroft, John Gielgud. (co-director: Anthony Quayle)

APPENDIX 3

THE WAY OF THE WORLD	Lyric, Hammersmith, 1924.
Millamant	Edith Evans
Mirabel	Robert Loraine
Lady Wishfort	Margaret Yarde
Witwoud	Nigel Playfair

	Lyric, Hammersmith, 1953.
Millamant	Pamela Brown
Mirabel	John Gielgud
Lady Wishfort	Margaret Rutherford
Witwoud	Paul Scofield

LOVE FOR LOVE	Playhouse, Oxford, 1924.
Valentine	John Gielgud
Tattle	W. Earle Grey
Angelica	Flora Robson
Scandal	Peter Creswell
Foresight	Richard Goolden
Mrs Frail	Mary Grey
Mrs Foresight	Molly McArthur
Ben	R. S. Smith
Sir Sampson	Reginald Denham

Phoenix, 1943, and Haymarket, 1944.

Valentine	John Gielgud
Tattle	Leslie Banks
Angelica	Rosalie Crutchley
Scandal	Leon Quartermaine
Foresight	Miles Malleson
Mrs Frail	Adrianne Allen
Mrs Foresight	Marian Spencer
Ben	George Woodbridge
Sir Sampson	Cecil Trouncer

The Royale, New York, 1947

Valentine	John Gielgud
Tattle	Cyril Ritchard
Angelica	Pamela Brown
Scandal	George Hayes
Foresight	John Kidd
Mrs Frail	Yvonne Arnaud
Mrs Foresight	Marian Spencer
Ben	Robert Flemyng
Sir Sampson	Malcolm Keen

THE BEGGAR'S OPERA	Theatre Royal, Haymarket, 1940.
Macheath	Michael Redgrave
Polly Peachum	Audrey Mildmay
Lucy Lockit	Linda Gray
Peachum	Roy Henderson

THE SCHOOL FOR SCANDAL
(Chapter 8)

THE SCHOOL FOR SCANDAL	Queen's Theatre, London, 1937.
Sir Peter Teazle	Leon Quartermaine
Lady Teazle	Peggy Ashcroft
Joseph Surface	John Gielgud
Charles Surface	Michael Redgrave
Mrs Candour	Athene Seyler

Theatre Royal, Haymarket, 1962.

Sir Peter Teazle	Ralph Richardson
Lady Teazle	Anna Massey
Joseph Surface	John Neville
Charles Surface	Daniel Massey
Mrs Candour	Margaret Rutherford

Majestic Theatre, New York, 1963.

Sir Peter Teazle	Ralph Richardson
Lady Teazle	Geraldine McEwan
Joseph Surface	John Gielgud
Charles Surface	Richard Easton
Mrs Candour	Gwen Ffrangcon-Davies

THE IMPORTANCE OF BEING EARNEST
(Chapter 9)

THE IMPORTANCE OF
BEING EARNEST

The Globe, 1939.

John Worthing	John Gielgud
Algernon Moncrieff	Ronald Ward
Gwendolen Fairfax	Joyce Carey
Cecily Cardew	Angela Baddeley
Lady Bracknell	Edith Evans
Miss Prism	Margaret Rutherford
Rev. Canon Chasuble	David Horne

The Globe, 1941.

John Worthing	John Gielgud
Algernon Moncrieff	Jack Hawkins
Gwendolen Fairfax	Gwen Ffrangcon-Davies
Cecily Cardew	Peggy Ashcroft
Lady Bracknell	Edith Evans
Miss Prism	Margaret Rutherford
Rev. Canon Chasuble	George Howe

Phoenix, 1942.

John Worthing	John Gielgud
Algernon Moncrieff	Cyril Ritchard
Gwendolen Fairfax	Gwen Ffrangcon-Davies
Cecily Cardew	Peggy Ashcroft
Lady Bracknell	Edith Evans
Miss Prism	Jean Cadell
Rev. Canon Chasuble	J. H. Roberts

Royale, New York, 1947.

John Worthing	John Gielgud
Algernon Moncrieff	Robert Flemyng
Gwendolen Fairfax	Pamela Brown
Cecily Cardew	Jane Baxter
Lady Bracknell	Margaret Rutherford
Miss Prism	Jean Cadell
Rev. Canon Chasuble	John Kidd

APPENDIX 4

THE (1924) Playhouse, Oxford. Lyric, Hammersmith.
CHERRY ORCHARD   Royalty, London.

Director, J. B. Fagan
Trofimov   John Gielgud
Madame Ranevsky   Mary Grey
Gaev   Alan Napier
Firs   Richard Goolden
Lopahin   Fred O'Donovan

(1954) Lyric, Hammersmith.
Directed and text adapted by John Gielgud
Madame Ranevsky   Gwen Ffrangcon-Davies
Gaev   Esmé Percy
Firs   Hugh Pryse
Lopahin   Trevor Howard

(1961) Aldwych Theatre, London.
Director, Michel Saint-Denis
Madame Ranevsky   Peggy Ashcroft
Gaev   John Gielgud
Firs   Roy Dotrice
Lopahin   George Murcell

THE SEAGULL	(1925)	Arts and Little Theatre, London.

Director, A. E. Filmer

Constantin	John Gielgud
Madame Arkadina	Miriam Lewes
Nina	Valerie Taylor
Trigorin	Randolph McLeod

(1936) New Theatre, London.

Director and adapter, Theodore
Komisarjevsky

Trigorin	John Gielgud
Madame Arkadina	Edith Evans
Nina	Peggy Ashcroft
Constantin	Stephen Haggard

THE THREE SISTERS	(1925)	Barnes Theatre, London.

Director, Theodore Komisarjevsky

Tusenbach	John Gielgud
Vershinin	Ion Swinley
Olga	Mary Sheridan
Masha	Beatrix Thomson
Irina	Margaret Swallow
Natasha	Dorice Fordred

(1938) Queen's Theatre, London.

Director, Michel Saint-Denis

Tusenbach	Michael Redgrave
Vershinin	John Gielgud
Olga	Gwen Ffrangcon-Davies
Masha	Carol Goodner
Irina	Peggy Ashcroft
Natasha	Angela Baddeley

INDEX